Pains For A Purpose

Pains For A Purpose

By

Cecil E. Howard

Sula Too Publishing

Copyright © 2019, 2021 Cecil E. Howard All rights reserved. This book may not be reproduced in whole or in part without written permission from the copyright holder, except by a reviewer who may quote brief passages in a review; nor may any part of this book be reproduced, stored in retrieval system, or transmitted in any form or by any means, electronic, mechanical, photocopying, recording, or other, without prior written permission from the copyright holder.

ISBN-13: 978-1-7339542-0-4 Paperback

Library of Congress Control Number: 2019909727

Memoir

Printed and bound in the United States of America
October 2021
10 9 8 7 6 5 4 3 2

Vintage cover photo Library of Congress, Prints & Photographs Division, FSA/OWI Collection

Published by
Sula Too Publishing
Tampa, Florida
www.sulatoo.com/publishing

Dedication

This book is lovingly dedicated to my mother, Catherine Howard, who has resided in Heaven since July 1, 2008. Despite the challenges, struggles and setbacks she faced while raising four boys, she gave her best effort and never gave into the pressures. Her strength and determination have been my constant reminder during the process of writing this book.

Contents

Motivation	13
Beginnings	19
Danger	24
Lessons	29
Death	34
Survival	40
Life	44
Pop	50
Poison	59
Mr. Crews	65
A Lesson Learned	70
Uncle John	75
Adolescence	78
Integration	86
Hustling	91
Gator	99
Liberty City	106
Becoming Disabled	116
Jake and the Big Green Monster	120
Man of the House	131
Life in the City	139
Pro Football	144
Making Moves	147
Florida State	155
Pledging	165
Finding Salvation	172
Navigating College	179
Priscilla	185
Chief	195
Law School Acceptance	197
Graduation	200
Reflections	206
Epilogue	210

Acknowledgements

Great love and appreciation are extended to my beautiful and loyal wife Priscilla, who not only encouraged me to write this book, but has been my soul-mate, friend, and biggest supporter in every endeavor I've chased throughout our relationship. She is indeed, bone of my bone.

Acknowledgements are in order for all of those young men and women who were raised in environments that were seemingly not conducive to effective learning and wellbeing, but found the will to survive, thrive, and return to help others. There are so many, yet their quiet work goes unnoticed.

Sincerest appreciation is extended to each of the five pastors I've had in my Christian lifetime, Moses General Myles (R.I.P.), Joseph Ratliff, R. B. Holmes, Jr., Adrian S. Taylor and Larry Roundtree II. Each of them has been highly impactful in teaching me God's Mighty Word, and its applicability in my life. Were it not for those five men, I'm not sure this book would have been written.

Appreciation is extended to my Alpha Phi Alpha Fraternity brothers who became family members at a time when I desperately needed strong familial relationships. They exposed me to Christianity, unity, laughter, brotherly love, and a strong sense of self-esteem that has sustained me over a lifetime.

Finally, appreciation is extended to my close friends whom I referenced in this book, mostly via pseudonyms. They helped to shape my young life in ways I could never have imagined. You know who you are.

Introduction

This book is more than 30 years in the making. It chronicles my life up to age twenty-one in a way that I would have never imagined. Being a generally private person, I've never let too many people get beyond the proverbial arm's reach parameters of my protected space.

During my early dating years with my wife, she and I would sit up all night long talking about our lives, our families, our friends, and our future. I exposed my secret world to her more than I had done with anyone else, but even then, it was a story here or a story there depending on the subject matter we were discussing. Over the years, I began telling the same stories over and over again, and she would promptly remind me that she had heard particular stories before. Sometimes, she would even complete the story for me.

Those early years of us telling each other our stories is what made me fall in love with her. I would often say, "Finally, I feel comfortable laying all this stuff on someone."

Despite my opening the vault to my early years, I still don't believe I've told my wife everything, because there is so much that I deemed worthy of disclosing that after thirty-five years of marriage still had not been shared, or at least, still hadn't been shared a second or third time such that she would remember.

One night while discussing a crazy incident from my youth, my wife stated to me that I should write a book of my life. My first impression was there was absolutely no way

I'd open my private life to everyone on the planet! After I came out of that convulsive thought, I then thought there was nothing too significant about my early life that strangers or even acquaintances would find interesting. In fact, I felt the average kid growing up in poverty in urban America probably experienced many of the same woes I encountered.

The conversations between the two of us about telling my story went on for many years, and over time, the prospect appeared to resonate with me more and more, especially after raising children. Of course, during those child-raising years, I was constantly reminded about my youth, but I was careful to make sure my children's youthful years were completely void of my unfortunate experiences. From time to time, I'd give my children a glimpse into my past as I discussed certain anecdotes that may have been relevant to particular situations we were discussing.

As I gave more and more thought to writing this book, I discovered a purpose beyond just entertaining people with a good story. It dawned on me that there were millions of children in poverty in this twenty-first century who desperately wanted out of their situations, but lacked the skills to efficiently navigate their courses. And, in an effort to use street skills to achieve some measure of success, the proliferation of criminal activity, school under performance, or sexual promiscuity would drive them off course. Such frustration typically led to school dropout, incarceration, homelessness, sexually transmitted diseases, and mental health issues, to name a few.

In many instances, if they survived all of those atrocities, their children were typically raised by grandparents, other family members, or even unrelated neighbors. Those children oftentimes found themselves in the same cycle of poverty, miseducation, and hopelessness. I have literally seen and lived a part of these so-called "curses" that have persisted through multiple generations.

The more I looked back over the plight of my early years, as well as the misfortunes of so many hundreds of people I knew, and millions more I did not know, I decided I would tell my story to fuel three components. First, my desire is that young people read, discuss, and become inspired. It is important that they understand their current situations are not new and certainly are not permanent. Many studies have shown that black children live in poverty at much higher rates than any other group, and they tend to remain there even into adulthood. For me, as I looked back over my family tree, I couldn't find wealth, property ownership, or even major educational achievements, and according to a survey sponsored by the Annie E. Casey Foundation, there was a 42% chance that even I would remain within a vicious cycle of poverty.

Young people need to see that others were in their same situations, but overcame their challenges through hard work, avoidance of continuous criminal activity, and pursuit of some aspect of educational achievement. Everybody does not have to go to college. In fact, college is not for everyone, but society has come to accept no less than a high school diploma or G.E.D. as a bottom-line standard that has to be attained for jobs, loans, and even respectability.

Secondly, this book is intended to educate the established guardians of the door to educational opportunities, jobs, home ownership, and financial opportunities. Too frequently, these guardians of the status quo make conclusions or assessments about people based on their past, or whatever stations of life they may have been stalled in, as opposed to giving serious consideration to individuals' potential.

I see this frequently in higher education, where in most instances, poverty-stricken youth with unfavorable backgrounds find themselves under performing in schools. They fall behind not because of aptitude, but because of ancillary factors such as hunger, illness, sexual and physical abuse, or bullying. Many colleges and universities, however, tend to ignore these facts. Instead, they tend to focus primarily on grades and standardized test scores. Many seem to have discontinued reliance upon personal statements and interviews as a way to get to know the type of students they accept. I firmly believe there are thousands of applicants every year who are summarily bypassed because of surface-level evaluations of their applications as opposed to serious assessments of factors in their background that reveal evidence of true grit and determination. The end result is typically acceptance of a homogeneous group of students with high grade point averages and test scores, but who graduate at less than favorable rates.

Lastly, I intend to focus on how God, my Heavenly Father, impacted my life in a magnificent way, how He was directing my path without my even knowing it, and how He blessed my family and me to the point that we were not consumed, when based upon all rational thought, we should have been consumed many times over.

For someone who grew up with no spiritual awareness, my amazing introduction to Christianity and knowledge of the power of God showed me how He had been in my life from day one without my ever knowing it. It's easy, albeit quite emotional, to look back during those years and see where God was working. Interestingly, He waited until I accepted Him in my life before He even started showing me what He was up to.

It is my personal hope that many will see themselves in specific aspects of my young life, as I don't believe I missed too many situations. As I read from one writer, I wouldn't believe my story had I not written it myself. Writing and reliving it was one of the most difficult things I've ever done. I cannot begin to describe the emotions that years of suppression brought about. I literally traveled the entire wheel of crying, cursing, screaming, laughing, worrying, sneering, and rejoicing, as I relived a very difficult time in my life. In the end, however, I encountered a form of therapy that no counselor or drug could have ever provided. It was a profound self-realization that my journey through hell was just a prep course for a greater and brighter future. The pains were indeed for a purpose.

Chapter 1

Motivation

The mid-August weather was hot and humid in Destin, a vacation resort town in the Florida panhandle, along the Gulf of Mexico, as my wife, Priscilla, and I celebrated our thirty-fourth wedding anniversary. Destin was our private getaway. We are not beach people per se, but we like vacationing in beach resorts and everything that comes with it. Destin was made for people like us. There are a lot of opportunities for shopping, outstanding restaurants, great wine spots, and complete peace of mind. In fact, I typically tell Priscilla, as we cross the bridge that takes us across the Choctawhatchee Bay into the Destin area, that all of my cares were left behind on the other side of the bridge.

On this particular three-day weekend trip, we walked a lot, ate a lot, drank a lot of wine, and more than any other time, watched a few hours of Netflix. We basically did whatever we wanted to do without any agenda whatsoever. It was the perfect weekend. We mingled with many other vacationers from other southeastern cities, such as Atlanta, Baton Rouge, Jackson, Birmingham, and Nashville. Sure, we could do all of that in our cosmopolitan city of Tampa, or in our other getaway city of St. Petersburg, however there was something special about doing it in Destin, the destination of many of our past family vacations, birthday celebrations, and holiday gatherings. That place has always been very special to my family and me. What a wonderful weekend it was.

Sometime during the weekend, we decided to watch a few episodes of a Netflix documentary that we had started enjoying a few days earlier back in Tampa. The documentary, entitled "Last Chance U" was about a junior college in rural Mississippi where college football players who had started their collegiate careers at major Division One programs, but left for a myriad of reasons, and found themselves at the junior college in an effort to resurrect their careers before going back to a Division One football program for their final years of college eligibility.

The documentary at that time was two seasons long and had about eight episodes for each season. We were sold after the second episode. So, while in Destin celebrating our anniversary, we decided to watch a few more episodes, and before we realized it, we had watched the entire first season. The documentary tended to focus on a few players each episode, possibly as a way to connect the viewers with each player's personality and background. This aspect took the movie out of the realm of a sports documentary and focused it more on the human element. It appeared that about 95%

of the featured players were black and many of them had experienced broken homes, foster care, murdered parents, drug usage, criminality, and extreme poverty. Further, much of their history contributed to their circumstances and their reasons for being at the junior college. Additionally, many of the young men and their coaches really did see their matriculation at the college as their last chance. Despite their good football talents, their only choices were to either be there in rural Mississippi getting a junior college degree or at home hanging out with the guys they grew up with and no prospects for bright futures.

As I viewed the documentary through tears, laughs, and football yelps, I started wondering what last chances the players were seeking. Was this truly their last chance at a potential football career? A college degree? A stable life? A life, period?

So many of the players' stories reminded me of the pain, sadness, and distress I experienced as a fatherless child growing up in Miami, Florida. Despite such daunting flashbacks, however, I continued watching episode after episode, even after Priscilla had gone to bed. Something kept me glued to the TV. Even though I was never much of an athlete, I saw a part of me in all of those young men. They were all missing something in life, but at the same time, chasing it with this supposed last chance. I was beyond intrigued. As I lay awake looking up at the ceiling that night, I couldn't help but continue wondering about those young men. Their lives were so real to me because the documentary was a true and accurate reflection of the lives they were actually living, and had lived. More importantly, it kept reminding me of the life I had lived as a youth.

Because I couldn't sleep, I finally got up and started watching another episode of the documentary, but by now, we had gone into the second season. Then, something happened to me. One of the players talked about how he and his other two brothers had grown up in foster care and after they became teens, the child welfare authorities wanted to split them up, but they resisted that effort and agreed that they would stick together no matter the circumstances. The player even brought his brother to college with him because he didn't want to leave him behind. That did it for me. My tear ducts just erupted. I just sat there in front of the television profusely crying while trying not to awaken Priscilla. Years of my early life flashed back. I thought of the hurt I endured as a young boy growing up in Miami, the things I wished for that never came true, and even the embarrassment of wanting to go to church, but did not have decent enough clothes to wear. I thought of all the people I knew who faced similar challenges. I felt I needed to reach out and do something, and at the same time, felt completely helpless.

I couldn't quite understand why I was crying. In fact, the older I get, the more I well up with tears whenever I see situations of young black men dealing with their struggles and trying in their own unsophisticated manner to exact various measures of resolution, which is so difficult to do. After a good cry, I finished watching the episode, but before I went back to bed, I prayed to God to equip me with the means and the knowledge to help my brothers in the struggle. My reference to "my brothers," meant my own blood brothers, nephews, and cousins who have endured struggles out of this world, but also the millions of young black men who could really use the help.

The next morning, I woke up with the enthusiasm of a child at Christmas and was determined to do whatever was necessary to make a greater contribution than I had been making toward easing the plight of my brothers. I resolved I needed to rid myself of the excuse that I was too busy, or that my little bit of help couldn't solve a much bigger problem. I had to make an impact. Doing so had always been important to me, but all of a sudden, it had become a matter of extreme urgency! During my adult life, I had created several formal mentoring programs and established thousands of informal mentoring and/or counseling relationships, but after my epiphany of sorts, I felt I needed to do more. My heart raced like it had not in years. Even during breakfast, I could not stop yapping to Priscilla that I had found my purpose in life. As usual, she sat back, listened, gave pointers, and then her blessing and support for me to go forward with whatever I thought was necessary to aid my brothers.

Later, after thinking more about the documentary, I started reflecting back on my younger years and all of the problems and vulnerabilities I encountered, and essentially suppressed inside a hard outer shell, but extremely vulnerable inner core. It made me realize that over my life, I had given so much of myself in the way of assuming responsibility, giving advice, providing mentoring, lending assistance, and loaning money, that I never took the time to seek out any of that on my own behalf. That's when I realized that's who I am. That's my purpose for being here. That's why I experienced the hard life, setbacks, and disappointments. I really think God was preparing me for a lifetime of benevolence and charity, and I'm not so sure I would have properly developed had I not experienced a life of hell during those developing years.

That life of hell prepared me for the person I have become, one who could not say "no" in even the most aggravating circumstances. I always felt I would hurt people's feeling by telling them no, and then I would agonize over it in hopes that they would ask again just so that I could redeem myself by adhering to their wishes.

Chapter 2

Beginnings

My father and mother grew up in Brooks County, Georgia, a small rural county on the northern Florida border. The county seat of Brooks County is Quitman, which is where the locals from the surrounding towns hung out, shopped, and paid their bills. Neither Mom nor Dad lived in Quitman. Mom and her family lived in a small wooden house in the back woods of an unincorporated area in the western portion of the county known as Dixie. Dad grew up with his seven sisters and two brothers in a modest wooden house in Morven, a town located in the northwest quadrant of the county. Mom was a mere teenager and Dad was barely twenty years old when they married; neither had finished high school. Shortly thereafter, Mom became pregnant with twin boys, and at age 20, she delivered Aaron and Abram without heartbeats in 1955. Sadly, my twin big brothers were stillborn. My sister Janice was born in 1956 and I came along in 1959. My second sister, Renee, came right on my heels in 1960.

Shortly after Renee's birth, and before Mom could have

another baby in Georgia, my dad did what many men in South Georgia did in those days. Due to racism and extremely low opportunities for decent jobs with good wages, he left the state and went to Miami to find work. There, he found a job as a truck driver and began his career driving long distances. While in Miami, my other three brothers, Tony, Darrell, and Travis were born in three consecutive years in 1963, 1964, and 1965. My nickname for them while growing up was the Three Stairsteps, although during their growing years, they did not resemble stairs according to their height. Tony was the tallest and actually outgrew me in height. Mom used to always say he resembled an uncle on Dad's side who I never got a chance to meet. Despite Darrell being the middle of the three, he grew much slower than anyone and ended up being the shortest of everybody, which contributed to his early nickname of "Coot." Travis, the baby, quickly outgrew Darrell, and according to Mom, he was the spitting image of Dad's older brother, Willie.

When the family got to Miami, we initially settled into an area of Miami known as Brown Sub that was inhabited almost exclusively by blacks. Mom was pregnant with Tony and did not work, but Dad's long-distance driving job adequately took care of the family. We lived in a community of duplex units with very low and flat rooftops. That description gave the community its name, the Flat Tops. It was the very first idea of community I knew. The neighbors all knew each other and the children all played outside in a big, open, grassy lot. Huge logs separated the grassy play area from the street and we kids knew our play boundary was on the grassy side of the logs and not the street side. Even if a ball went beyond the logs, we knew we couldn't get it. Instead, we had to go get an adult who had to come out and get it. Since the duplexes surrounded the grassy area, there was always an adult willing to come outside to get our balls.

Life was so simple and happy in the Flat Tops. Most of the families had a mother and father present in the two-bedroom units which consisted of a living room, kitchen, bathroom, and two bedrooms. Mom and Dad slept in one bedroom and we kids slept in the other. Although I was only four years old, the years spent living in the Flat Tops were very happy. I was very aware of my surroundings and I knew all of the neighbors and their children. The community seemed like one large family. I can't remember any strife or other controversies between the neighbors. In fact, the grown-ups usually congregated at each other's houses while we children played outside in the big grassy lot. They didn't worry about us too much because we all knew we had to stay on the grassy side of the big logs and not dare go near the streets.

I often look back on those years and marvel at how obedient we were. We had clearly defined boundaries and as small children, we strictly adhered to those boundaries. Part of the reason for our obedience was fear. Not fear of what our parents would do to us if we disobeyed them, but fear of what would happen to us beyond the logs. The grown-ups often told stories about white people who would kill or harm us if they caught us without our parents. This was the height of the civil rights era and as our parents congregated with other parents to drink, socialize, and discuss the latest incidents of violence by whites against blacks in the South, we couldn't help but buy into the fear they had planted in our minds. We may have been mere young children but we all had been thoroughly prepared and all of us were very alert to our surroundings, to constantly point out things that seemed suspicious.

By the time I turned five, I could tell that I was the apple of my daddy's eye. I don't recall him interacting too much with my two sisters or my baby brother, Tony. In fact, I distinctly remember Janice, though three years older than me, being quite timid and shy around Dad. If she wanted something from him, she would ask me to ask him. I, however, was Dad's big boy, and I could tell he looked as much forward to coming home to take me for rides in his big truck as I did. It was a true badge of honor for me to go off with him when the others had to stay home. It was the first time in my life I ever felt special and privileged.

Hanging out with Dad also had some not-so-good twists. During some of our rides, he took me to his girlfriend's house on the other end of the Flat Tops. I knew the girlfriend and I believed Mom knew her as well. I also knew her kids. Interestingly, I knew enough to understand that Dad was cheating on Mom and that I could not say a thing to Mom. I knew what Dad was doing was wrong, but he told me I could not say one word to anybody at all. Dad was larger than life to me, and at such an early age, I completely worshipped him to no end. There was absolutely no way anybody in the world could have forced that secret out of me. There was never a thought in my mind that I might spill the beans.

There were also a couple of other not so good things about Dad. He drank scotch liquor, and on some occasions when he drank, I could hear him and Mom fighting inside their bedroom. First they would begin arguing about Dad's visits to the other woman's house. I would hear Mom say, "Yeah, I know you keep going by that heifer's house. Everybody in town knows it." Fortunately, Mom never asked me about the visits, but even if she did, I would have honestly told her a huge lie and maintained the straightest face while doing so. Like clockwork, the arguing would then escalate to a point that Mom and Dad would start physically fighting. The house was not large at all, so it didn't take much to hear what was going on. At least they tried to keep their situation from us kids by closing their bedroom door. I never saw the actual fighting, but the sounds clearly indicated physical violence was happening. At age five, I could never understand the reason for the fighting, but I blamed it on the scotch, a drink I vowed to never drink. Although I have drank or tasted most types of alcohol in my 60 years, I still have never, ever tasted or desired to taste scotch, and each time I see it, I think back to those days when Dad and Mom used to fight.

In my young mind, the whiskey brought on the fighting, the fighting brought on Mom's leaving Dad, and her leaving eventually brought about Dad's death. As I grew older, I tended to separate those lines of thought, but as a young kid, my rationale was as solid as anything else.

Chapter 3

Danger

One of my greatest fears during my early years was the night my family lived through a major hurricane that hit Miami. Mom and Dad and all the grown-ups kept talking about somebody named Cleo, but I couldn't understand all the commotion and anxiety about this Cleo person until Dad finally made it clear that Cleo was a storm that could kill us. Mom and Dad anxiously packed Vienna sausages, sardines and crackers into the kitchen cabinet on the advice of neighbors because they were afraid we would lose electricity, and because we were located in the black neighborhood, the neighbors feared we would go weeks before getting the electricity restored, and most certainly after it was restored for the whites.

By the time Hurricane Cleo hit Miami, Mom and Dad had piled all of us into their bedroom, with a strong demand that we were to sit still and be quiet. Once the strong winds started howling and heavy rains started pelting our flat rooftop and windows, the fear became real. I looked to Mom and Dad for confirmation that everything would be alright, but I could barely make out their faces, because the electricity had gone out, and we were using a kerosene lamp for light. I recall Mom being very uncomfortable because she was pregnant with my brother Darrell. Dad, obviously frustrated by everything that was going on, kept assuring us that everything would be okay as long as we kept still and shut up. Despite his anxiety-filled assurances, I was as scared as I had ever been. The noise outside was too great for me to sit calmly. Then, all of a sudden, we all heard breaking glass. Something caused the window in our living room to break, which allowed water to enter our house. Dad then took a mattress from one of our beds and propped it up against the window in order to limit the amount of water entering the house. Although I was just a mere kid, I was very afraid that we would all die that night. Finally, amidst my quiet cry and nervousness, I drifted off to sleep while Cleo continued her assault on our house.

The morning after Cleo's punch, I awakened to Mom and Dad sweeping and mopping away water that had entered our house overnight. We didn't have to move out of our home, but water was everywhere. After a full day of cleaning up in Cleo's aftermath, things went back to normal in the Flat Tops.

Soon after Cleo's terror, Mom's youngest sister, Aunt Faye, moved to Miami. As a child, I believed Aunt Faye to be incredibly pretty. She was tall, caramel-colored women with striking features, and always wore a highly fashionable wig. I loved Aunt Faye as if she was my mother. She had no problem finding a job on Miami Beach, working as a live-in housekeeper for a Jewish family. She would ride the bus to the Flat Tops to stay with us on the weekends and return to her job on Monday mornings. Some of my fondest memories centered around us kids running to greet Aunt Faye as she got off the city bus on Friday afternoons and walked toward our house. She would always bring us goodies from the family she worked for, including used toys and hand-me-down clothes that the Jewish kids no longer wore. And, no matter what, she always carried a large wig box that contained her stylish wig. Like Dad and Mom, Aunt Faye was also an alcohol drinker, and I would often see her hiding a bottle of her own private vodka around the house.

One day, after Aunt Faye arrived, she and Mom were in Mom's bedroom chatting about a fifth of vodka that Aunt Faye brought with her. I watched as Aunt Faye and Mom both took a drink from a large bottle and placed it in the top drawer of Mom's dresser. Later that day, Mom and Dad left for an outing and Aunt Faye had the responsibility of babysitting us children, while she hosted a date. I recall most of us children being outside in the large grassy lot just playing around. I had been playing with my sister, Renee, and another girl, but after a few minutes, I left them and went into the house, walking past Aunt Faye and her date as they chatted, and walked into Mom's bedroom and retrieved the bottle of vodka from her dresser drawer, and took a swig. I drank the vodka straight out of the bottle as I had seen Mom and Aunt Faye do, and I actually liked the taste. A few minutes later, I made another trip to Mom's bedroom, and repeated the act of taking a swig of vodka from the bottle. As Aunt Faye and her date chatted in the living room, I made at least five or six trips past them into Mom's bedroom.

After my fifth or sixth trip to the vodka bottle, I knew something was wrong. I started feeling very strange, and could not comprehend what was happening to me, other than the fact that everything became blurred, and seemed to spin at a rapid pace. I always listened to adults' conversations, which in many instances centered around drinking alcohol, and I had often heard of stories of people being drunk, and had actually seen people pointed out as being drunk, but I never knew what that really meant until I reached that state. I walked past Aunt Faye and her date one last time, but could not know what type of shape I must have been in. Neither she nor her date stopped me or said anything to me. In fact, I'm not sure if they even noticed the number of times I walked past them, or that I was seriously imbibing in the stashed vodka.

Once outside, I ran back over to where Renee and her friend were playing to alert them that something was wrong. When they saw me running toward them, they began running away as if we were playing a "catch me if you can" game that we often played. I was not playing at that particular time. I needed their help as I ran after them screaming "I'm drunk, I'm drunk!" Despite my screams, Renee and her friend continued running with me right behind them.

At some point the chase ended as I must have fallen down and blacked out. I woke up the next morning at the hospital where Mom and Dad explained that I had been poisoned by the alcohol, had blacked out, and had to have the alcohol pumped from my stomach. I explained to them what I had done, and how I got the alcohol. I guess they were too relieved to get upset with me. Instead, Dad took his frustrations out by arguing with Mom right there at the hospital, but the nurse quickly quieted them.

After a doctor came to check me out, he told Mom and Dad that I was okay, did not appear to have any after-effects of the alcohol poisoning, and more importantly, that I could go home. Needless to say, I learned my lessons about the dangers of alcohol and I learned it the hard way.

During the drive home, Dad and Mom began arguing again about Mom and Aunt Faye having alcohol in my presence and leaving it where I could get it. I remember thinking at age five how alcohol was again playing a negative role between Mom and Dad even though it was strictly my fault that I intentionally snuck into and out of Mom's room on several instances to drink the alcohol.

Chapter 4

Lessons

Although Dad wasn't highly educated, he taught me some serious lessons early in my life that stayed with me forever. He always said to be careful of strangers, and if someone tried to talk to me and I didn't know them, to run away as quickly as possible. That lesson was universal in the Flat Tops, especially, since we children played outside by ourselves without adult supervision almost 100% of the time. His second lesson was that if someone bothered me and I couldn't protect myself, to pick up something and "knock the hell out of them." Those were great lessons, and for whatever reason, I was forced to use them very early.

Sometime during the summer before I started first grade, several of us children were playing in the large grassy lot when we noticed an older white man drive up to the big logs that separated the grassy area and the street. As he exited his car, he stood on the side of the big logs nearest the street while we kids stayed on the grassy area on the other side of the logs. We had never really seen a white man in our neighborhood, so we were quite curious as to the reason for his visit. He told us he was looking for his dog that had run away. Since we had been warned about whites on many occasions, we kept our distance while telling him we had not seen the dog he described. Then surprisingly a dollar bill dropped from his body and landed on the grassy side of the log while he stood near the street side. We were all between the ages of five and eight, but we all instantly knew the dollar drop was a trap, as we had heard of countless stories where white men were kidnapping small black children while using money to lure them close enough to be grabbed. Initially, none of us moved closer to the stranger. I, however, did have plans to get the dollar bill even though I knew the old man was using it as a trap. After he described his dog a bit more, I moved closer as if to hear him a little better. When I got close enough, I quickly snatched the dollar bill from the ground and dashed off while screaming to the other kids to run, run, run! I'm not sure whether it was fear, or just the experience of running everywhere I went, but I ran so hard and fast at that moment, that I barely felt my bare feet touch the ground. I knew if the strange man chased us, he'd come for me since I had the dollar bill. I also knew the consequences of me being caught would be dire, so I continued running as fast as my body would carry me, not knowing whether the stranger was chasing us or not.

All of us knew our environment very well. We knew the nooks, crannies, and vacant units where we could take short cuts. We knew we had to get to a safe place as quickly as possible, in case the strange man decided to pursue us. We knew he could not follow us in his car because the big logs prevented him from driving onto the grassy area where we were located. But, there was a chance he could drive around the block, park somewhere, and catch us on the other side. As a result, I told the other kids to follow me to the safety of Mom and Dad.

Mom and Dad were visiting another couple a few doors from our house. As we kids frantically burst into the neighbor's house screaming all at the same time that a white man was trying to kill us, Dad and the other father quickly jumped to their feet and ran out to look for the man, but when they got to where everything happened, the man had left. That incident gave Dad and the other father a prime opportunity to reinforce the rule that we not talk to any strangers. I was feeling proud of myself that I had tricked the stranger and beat him out of his money. I expected my quest to be the talk of the Flat Tops, and how I would become a popular topic amongst the residents. Dad and the other father, however, were not amused or impressed that I had snatched the dollar bill, so instead of lifting me up and telling me how great I was, they both chided me that my actions were not smart, and that I could have easily been snatched up by the stranger. From that day forward, we never saw the strange white man, but keenly understood the protocol for future reference.

The second lesson was less dramatic, but much more painful. As a first grader at Earlington Heights Elementary School, I was often bullied, probably due to my small size.

The majority of my suffering came at the hands of one kid who was much bigger than me. After getting quite tired of his tactics, I finally complained to Dad that the fat kid constantly hit and harassed me during the quarter mile walk home from school. (During those days, everybody walked home from school.) This news upset Dad, as I knew it would, but it caused him to give me some excellent advice. He pointed his finger at me and said, "If that big bully bothers you again, pick up something and knock the hell out of him." The very next day while Dad's instructions were fresh in my mind, the bully kid harassed and hit me for no reason. Remembering Dad's directives, I picked up what appeared to be a piece of tree branch and hit the bully across his face, which caused him to fall back and stumble to the ground. The look on his face and the loud cries from his mouth sent a strong message that he would not get up and come charging toward me, but just in case he did, I held the small piece of limb like a baseball bat, as if to dare him to come near me. The embarrassment of being knocked down, coupled with the raucous laughter of the other kids walking along the same route, was just too much to bear. The big kid got up, dusted himself off, and issued a threat that he was going to punch me in the face the next day. To me, that was his clear sign of retreat. I was worried that he would rush and overpower me while I held the piece of limb in hand. When he wisely chose to not make the situation worse, I breathed a big sigh of relief knowing there probably would not be any more bullying that day. On the other hand, I felt a flash of confidence rush through my body that made me want to continue my short-lived conquest. I didn't want the thrill of victory to end so quickly! I had successfully challenged my biggest nemesis and I wanted to make sure I never suffered at his hands again.

Later that afternoon, the bully's mom came to our house and had a discussion with Mom. I don't recall any consequences resulting from that visit; neither was I bullied by the big kid again. I adhered to that valuable lesson of survival throughout my youth, and as a result, never encountered too much harassment from larger kids, or other bullies.

Chapter 5

Death

Within two years after the move to Miami, Mom and Dad split up. In those days, many blacks did not get divorces; they just split up and went their separate ways, but remained married forever. That was the plan for Mom and Dad. They split without a plan to get divorced. I suspected the split up had something to do with Dad's female friend, Annie, who he stepped out to see from time to time, because I heard her name mentioned during Mom's and Dad's arguments.

One day, a large dark-skinned man named George came to the house and Mom packed all of us into his car. We moved to his apartment across town to an area of Miami known as Overtown. The entire area seemed to be dominated by two and three-story apartment buildings made of concrete and painted in dull blues, greens, browns, and pinks. Each complex had its own asphalt parking lot in front that doubled as the children's playground. George lived in a small one-bedroom apartment on the first floor. He and mom slept inside the bedroom, while my siblings and I (except Janice) slept on a pull-out couch in the living room. Janice was in Georgia at the time, having remained there when Dad took us there to visit his mother on an earlier trip. She became ill during our stay, and Dad left her there with Grandma Susie Lee with plans to bring her home after his next trip to Georgia.

Apparently, Dad's and Mom's split was real, because Dad would come over to George's apartment to see us kids on Fridays after work. Usually, he'd take us to get ice cream and bring us back. Travis, the baby, was only about two years old at the time, and because he was so young, Mom never let him go with us.

One Friday, that summer, Dad came over to the apartment to see us. As he usually did, he drove right up to the front of the first-floor apartment and we all ran out in an euphoric state to greet him. Mom came out as well with Travis in her arms, while George sat at the kitchen table that was pushed up against the window and could see everything that was going on outside. As we were piling into the car, Dad told Mom he wanted Travis to come along. Mom objected and stated it was time for Travis' bath. Dad became upset that Mom never let Travis go with us to get ice cream, so he attempted to grab Travis from Mom's arms, but Mom held on and pulled Travis back toward her.

When George saw what was going on, he jumped up, grabbed a knife from the utensil drawer and ran outside. As George came outside with an enraged look on his face, I shouted, "Daddy, George got a knife!" At that point Dad loosened his grip on Travis and started running, with George chasing right behind him. Mom quickly ushered us inside with usual instructions that I watch my brothers and sister and went running off behind George and Dad.

We went inside, but Renee and I watched from the same window that George had been peering from only moments earlier. Suddenly, I saw Dad run back toward his car, but then as if he had been lying in wait, George appeared out of nowhere, and charged at Dad. The two violently fought while George still held the knife in his hand. Then suddenly Dad bent over while grabbing his stomach area, and then fell to the ground. George went running off away from the apartment building. All of a sudden, time literally froze for me. I froze! I was only awakened from the horror of what I had just seen when I heard Mom screaming, "Oh Lord, he done killed my husband! Oh Lord, he done killed my husband!"

I was only seven years old, but was completely stunned to have witnessed my father's murder in cold blood. At that point, I had never experienced anyone dying. I couldn't understand it, but to hear my mother's frantic wails sent a shiver down my back that I will never forget. It told me that something was horribly wrong. Wrong and final. I immediately forgot my responsibility to watch my younger siblings and rushed outside to the crowd that had gathered around my fallen father. As I pushed through, I could see Dad on the ground with his eyes wide open, but he was very still. Blood was everywhere, and even more horrifying, I could literally see parts of his insides on the outside of his body on top of his stomach area. Mom was by his side on her knees still screaming that her husband had been killed. At that precise moment, the weight of the world fell upon my shoulders.

There I was at seven years old standing in the midst of a crowd watching my Dad's mutilated and slain body lie there on the hot summer concrete with throngs of onlookers commenting about losing their appetites and Mom screaming about her husband having been killed. I just stood there not knowing what to do or say, or where to even go. A feeling came over me that I had never experienced before, although in years later, I would experience it again. Finally, a neighbor grabbed my hand and took me back inside the apartment. She then found my younger siblings inside Dad's car hoping for our Friday ride to get ice cream. She explained that there would be no ice cream that day and ushered all of us back inside the apartment.

After what seemed like too long of a time, the police and then the ambulance came to the apartment building. The sound of the ambulance's siren made everyone scramble as the vehicle forced its way to get where my father's still body laid. After the longest time, the two guys in the ambulance put Dad's body onto a stretcher, covered him completely, and drove off.

Mom returned to the apartment crying while telling us our father was gone forever and we would not be able to see him again. We all cried, but for different reasons. Renee and I cried because Mom was crying, and she and I both feared George would come back to harm us. The younger siblings cried because there would be no ice cream that day.

A few days after Dad's murder, Mom took me with her to the funeral home, located about four blocks from the apartment. Once inside, we were directed to a chapel where I saw Grandma Susie Lee and Dad's two brothers Willie and Ray. There were a few others whom I did not know. Dad was lying in a casket at the front of the chapel, and all of the adults just sort of sat quietly without saying too much or too loudly. There was, however, light discussion about what happened, and I attempted to offer my very clear facts while understanding that not one adult in that room saw how the murder occurred. As adults typically did in those days, they told me to be quiet, and to go outside. I immediately went outside and sat on one of the curb stops outside the funeral home, and recall being angry about not being able to tell my story about Dad's death. I had heard the small talk inside the funeral chapel about Mom being the cause for Dad's death, and I desperately wanted to clear her name. Nobody had any interest in hearing it, as if I was too young to have understood what I saw and felt.

I could not understand the first death I experienced. I could not understand the finality, the pain, the grief. As I sat outside the funeral chapel, all I felt was a strange void inside me. There was no emotion at all; just a big ugly void. Why did this happen? What would happen to us? I was scared as I pondered whether George would come back and kill the rest of us. Finally, my far-off gaze was interrupted by Mom coming out of the chapel. She grabbed my hand and pulled me along as we walked back home. I could tell she was angry, but she didn't say too much other than utter a few incoherent statements to herself. She later told me that Dad's body was shipped back to Georgia for the funeral. Other than my oldest sister Janice who was still in Georgia, none of us, including Mom, attended the funeral. Once Mom and I left the funeral home that August evening, that was the last she or I ever saw of Dad.

All I had ever known, heard, or seen of Dad became locked in the vault of my mind never to be discussed with anyone. Neither Mom, nor anyone else, ever discussed the matter in my presence again. Maybe they thought I was too young to comprehend what happened. After all, it could be risky to trust the memory and accuracy of a seven-year-old. Everything was so clear that I can even recall a teenager standing in the crowd saying she had lost her appetite for a hamburger at a particular hamburger joint. In fact, for the longest time, I would not eat at that particular hamburger chain because of the memory of that dreadful day.

There is no experience like seeing a close family member murdered in cold blood right before your eyes, especially when the effects are tremendously grotesque like what I experienced. The scenery, the sounds, the smells, everything freezes in your brain. Strangely, the passage of time does very little to diminish the accuracy of what the senses experienced. If I live to be one hundred and seven years old, I will still recall with accuracy what I saw on that fateful August afternoon in 1967.

Chapter 6

Survival

At age 32 with five kids aged seven, six, four, three, and two, plus a 10-year-old who was living in Georgia with Grandma Susie Lee, Mom had to do a lot of things quickly. Dad was gone and George had fled, never to be heard from again. We were all alone and Mom was not only uneducated and inexperienced, she had never run a household full of small kids all by herself. Despite that, she was able to find a job at a hotel down the street while I watched my younger siblings with a stern warning from her to not go outside unless it was to go next door to Miss Rita's house for an emergency. Since it was still summer, none of us had to go to school, so we just stayed inside the apartment and played all day until Mom returned home. We were surrounded by people who knew us and who would waste no time putting a belt to our behinds if we got out of order and we were keenly aware of that fact.

At age seven, I had to grow up and become the man of the house. I was fully taking care of four younger siblings, including keeping everyone inside the apartment and making sure we all ate breakfast and lunch each day. I had watched Mom cook, so I had a general idea of how to cook easy stuff. And since we had started receiving food from "The Welfare," each box or can of food was clearly and boldly marked, "Milk," "Powdered Eggs," "Corn Flakes," "Meat," "Peanut Butter," and so forth. Basically, whatever was not ready to eat, I only had to mix with water for preparation. Peanut butter and jelly sandwiches were our favorite. The canned meat was another favorite. It was similar to what most people know as Spam. Mom would fry it in an open pan on top of the stove, and I learned to do the same thing. That was good eating! We didn't take too kindly to the powdered milk and eggs, but we consumed both when we were hungry enough. We ate pretty good, thanks to the mysterious place known as "The Welfare." To this day, I still consider the welfare as being a place as opposed to a status.

  Although we could not go outside while Mom was at work, she never said we could not let other kids into our apartment. So, occasionally we would let a few of the kids inside to play hide and seek. On one occasion, one of the girls grabbed my hand and told me to hide in the closet with her. She was about a year older than me and was the one who loved playing hide and seek the most. During one instance while we were in the closet, she unzipped my pants and started fondling me. She then took my hand and placed it under her dress. Our hands-only exploration of each other went on for a few minutes until that round of the game ended. No one discovered us, so we got to hide again during the next game.

During the second game, we did the same thing. She unzipped me and fondled me while guiding my hand under her dress. During that second game, one of the younger kids found us, and I was sure the kid saw what was going on. From that day forward, the other kids were not allowed in the apartment when Mom was at work.

About a week after the hide and seek incident, Mom came into the apartment and went straight to where she kept her belt. She then went straight to me and started beating with it. In between hits, she asked what the hell was I doing with a girl in the closet. Between screams and jumps, I pleaded with Mom that I did nothing, and that the girl guided and placed my hand under her dress. Mom said that sounded crazy and swung the belt even harder. After what seemed like hours, but in actuality, only five minutes, Mom stopped to rest. I took that opportunity to mercifully plead my case to her that I had nothing to do with that situation, but instead was led by an older girl. Maybe, I should have kept my mouth closed and let the process end, but I was intent on proclaiming my innocence. Further, my efforts at explanation only prompted Mom to give me a few more hits with the belt. I finally smartened up, and just took the beating, because the more I attempted to explain, the angrier Mom seemed to become. Finally, Mom stopped the beating, and left me in the room to cry my sorrows away. Needless to say, we never let another person inside the apartment while Mom was away.

By the time the school year started, Mom had started receiving social security benefits as a result of Dad's death.

One check was to her personally, and the other was for us, his children. I never could understand why Social Security sent two separate checks, but we were happy nonetheless that the checks were coming. This monthly benefit totaled approximately $500, and allowed Mom to move us from George's apartment, to another apartment building a few blocks down the street, but still in the Overtown section of Miami. Since George was on the run, I finally stopped worrying about him returning, and we eventually adjusted to our new surroundings.

During that first year and half on our own, we managed pretty well with the social security and welfare benefits. I was now in second grade at Douglas Elementary School, my new school, and Renee had just started first grade, after not attending kindergarten. I did the exact thing when I started first grade at Earlington Heights Elementary a year earlier.

Chapter 7

Life

I've always had a special affinity for schools. I'm not sure if I just liked learning, or whether I saw school as an escape from the pressures of trying to survive. There was always some magnetic force within me when it came to schools. I preferred being there compared to anywhere else. So, during the summer after second grade, two buddies from the apartments and I found ourselves at our school. None of us attended summer school, but we wanted to see what this whole summer school thing was about. Mom was no longer working at the hotel, so I didn't have to babysit all day long. I could roam the streets of Overtown, bare footed like all the other kids. The place was a hot, concrete jungle with small rocks and pieces of glass everywhere, but over time, the soles of our bare feet were able to withstand the severe poundings we put on them as we got into mischief.

On this day, we went to Douglas Elementary and found an unlocked window to one of the classrooms. Since summer school had let out for the day, we climbed through the open window into the classroom. Although we weren't looking for anything in particular, we felt it necessary to rummage through loads of paper, crayons, chalk, and other school supplies that were neatly packed on the shelves. We figured we'd take our find back to the apartments and play school, which was one of my favorite pastimes. Little did we know, a janitor had detected us. When he opened the door to the classroom, we panicked before using the second door of the classroom as an escape route to get out of the school and make a hasty retreat to the apartments some four blocks away. The janitor chased us, but our speed, street smarts, and familiarity with the community was just too much for the poor guy. There was no way he would ever catch us! He finally gave up trying, but not before screaming that he would beat the hell out of us if he caught our "lil roguish butts" around there again.

In those days, there was an unspoken rule that grown-ups could discipline or "chastise" children if they caught them doing mischievous things. We knew if the janitor caught us, he would put his belt to our behinds, and if we reported to our parents what happened, they would beat us a second time. So, normally, we'd take the whipping if we were caught, and not say anything else about it to anyone. The janitor apparently recognized all of us, and within a day or so, someone from the school came to the apartments to talk to our mothers about our little burglary situation.

Mom was advised that we would be punished when we returned to school in the Fall. Fortunately for me, or maybe unfortunately, we had moved back to Brown Sub just before summer ended and Mom ended up re-enrolling me at Earlington

Heights for third grade, the same school I started first grade just two years earlier. I didn't last long there, because Mom had issues with paying rent, and we had to move to another house in Brown Sub. The move necessitated another change of schools. This time, it was Bethune Elementary. When I started there in mid-year, the third graders were learning how to spell three-letter words and other words that rhymed when the first letter was changed. For example, the word "cat" would change to "bat" by simply removing the "c" and replacing it with a "b." Looking back, our level of instruction was probably remedial in nature, but it felt, like I was really learning and not missing much due to the constant changes in my life.

Then one night, I heard Mom crying out as she returned home. She had received the social security checks earlier that day and had waited around for a friend to take her to the check cashing store. Mom never had a checking account. She always cashed her check at a check cashing business, paid the surcharge, and then paid her creditors with cash or money orders. On this occasion, a hoodlum waited outside for her to cash her checks and as soon as she walked outside the business, he snatched her purse with our entire month's survival inside.

When Mom's friend brought her to the house, it was dark outside and we children were all inside, as I was fully engaged in my caretaker duties while Mom was out of the house. Mom got out of the car wailing in a loud pitched voice. Initially, I couldn't understand what she was saying, but having heard a familiar cry from her when Dad was murdered, I rushed outside to see what was happening. When Mom saw me, all she could do was wail even louder as she dropped to her knees in an almost praying-like position while screaming, "Lord please help me! They snatched my pocketbook! They done took all the money I have."

As a poor family, we looked forward to the third day of the month when social security checks arrived in the mail. We knew as long as that check came, we'd continue to have a safe place to stay, have lights, and would be able to eat decently for a few days. Plus, we knew whenever Mom returned from cashing her check, she'd bring home a family-sized bucket of our favorite fried chicken for dinner. On this night, however, everything suddenly changed. My excited anticipation of Mom's return, coupled with the disastrous occurrence of events, ushered me into a state of shock. I just stood there stunned at what I was hearing. I wanted to do something but could not do anything at all. I felt completely helpless, as Mom called on the Lord, while her male friend just stood there helplessly looking at the drama and not saying anything, and my younger brothers and sister standing on the front porch taking it all in. I wondered what they were thinking. What were we going to do? Who could I call? What would we eat?

The real impact of the crime really hit me about two weeks later. As Renee and I walked home from school and got closer to our house, we could see Mom talking with a neighbor and holding her head in her hands. I wondered what was going on. Then, as we passed a pile of household furnishings and clothes sitting next to the street, I realized those were our belongings. Mom explained that she could not pay the rent and the landlord had the Sheriff to remove all of our belongings from the house onto the side of the street and padlocked the door. We retrieved what clothes we could and stayed with a neighbor for a few days.

As an eight-year-old, I had experienced many different kinds of emotions, but never had I experienced the feeling that raced through my body when I saw a pile of belongings on the side of the street that happened to belong to us. During that time, people in the poorer black communities would establish trash piles in front of their houses whereby they would dump trash and unwanted household items, and a city truck would come by periodically to retrieve the items for delivery to the city dump. Sometimes, the trash piles would exist for several weeks until the trucks came. The trash piles were a common sight, and sometimes, neighbors would rummage through whatever was placed in someone's pile in hopes of finding a treasure. Such treasures were indeed rare if they existed at all. The piles also commonly attracted rats, opossums, stray dogs and cats, and an occasional brown snake. We learned to stay away from the trash piles unless of course, we could identify something of value, such as a small, operable appliance, or furniture pieces that were not broken, or maybe an old toy that someone had outgrown.

Upon realizing the items were not a trash pile, but were in fact, our household items, I sensed a new level of fear that I had never felt. This fear was different than what I felt the night Hurricane Cleo pelted our house in the Flat Tops. It was also different than what I felt after Dad was murdered and George was on the loose. I immediately envisioned us living on the streets with no protection from the horrendous heat and rainstorms or persons who would do harm to us. I also envisioned us not having food, and actually having to rummage through the trash piles in hopes that someone may have dumped their garbage there, as some were prone to do.

    Just minutes prior, I was excited about the prospects of getting out of the hot sun, and into the comforts of our house, and then with the quickness of a flash, my patchwork of security was instantaneously stripped away. The pain, grief, and overall sheer helplessness that I immediately experienced from that horrific incident brought on an unexplainable silent rage, that I could not do anything about. I just stood there watching Mom cry, while Renee looked puzzled, and my younger brothers played outside completely oblivious to the fact that our lives were going down the drain. How I wished I were them at that precise moment. Instead, I was burdened with being the man of the house so to speak, and I knew Mom relied on my ability to carry that burden.

Chapter 8

Pop

After our forced eviction, Mom was able to borrow and beg for enough funds that allowed us to find another place to live in an area of Miami close to the Brown Sub section of town. This meant I would be transferring schools again in the middle of the school year. This time, the new school was Lorah Park Elementary, a relatively new school that was completely windowless. Instead of having separate classrooms, the school had large learning areas that were sectioned off into units that were known as pods. Uniquely, the pods were designated by the letters L,O, R, A, H, P and K. First graders were in Pod L; second graders were in Pod O; third graders were in Pod R, and so forth. We were told this was the classroom of the future and that eventually all schools would be built like Lorah Park. It was the coolest thing to me, because while sitting in class, you could easily look across the pods and see what else was going on, especially if two kids were fighting. Fights amongst the students were common, and sometimes we'd get lucky and see a student attempt to fight a teacher. In any event, the entire pod would become disrupted, which seriously hampered effective learning.

This latest move brought us to another one-bedroom apartment in Brown Sub. Although Floral Heights Elementary School was within a block of the apartments, Mom never took us out of Lorah Park which was about one mile away. So, at ages seven and eight, respectively, Renee and I walked back and forth along busy N.W. 54th Street for seven city blocks, which included crossing very busy and dangerous northwest 27th Avenue, in order to get to Lorah Park Elementary. Miraculously, we made that trek every day, without incident, even on rainy or cold days.

Since we didn't go to Floral Heights with all the other kids, we never really got to know them beyond the playtime we engaged in after we all got home from school. I always felt like we seemed weird to them. They would often ask us why we weren't attending their school, but we could never really give them a legitimate reason. They thought it was weird that we had to walk all the way to Lorah Park, which to them, seemed so far away. Still, we had no answers.

Finally, the weirdness was too much to bear for one of the older girls who was about ten years old, and who lived on the third floor in the apartments. Her constant questions gradually turned to derogatory statements about our appearance. On many occasions, she told me how dirty we were, or how bad we smelled, even when I knew our clothes and bodies were clean. In fact, because I knew I would face a daily inspection from her, I made sure I wore the cleanest play clothes I could find whenever I'd go outside to play. Despite that, the inspector girl constantly reminded me of how dirty and ragged our clothes were, or how bad we smelled. Her criticisms became so abusive that I started staying inside the apartment more frequently just to avoid her. To make matters worse, some of the other kids started doing the same thing she did. I was sure my appearance and body odor were not as the kids said, but for whatever reason, one by one, they fell in line with the inspector girl and mocked us.

During our stay at the apartments, we always had company. Usually, when Aunt Faye came over, she'd bring a friend with her. During one particular visit, she came over with a guy named Carl, and they took Mom to cash her social security checks and to go to the grocery store. When they returned, they also had a bottle of liquor and sat around and had drinks while I just hung out in the small one-bedroom apartment too embarrassed to play outside with the other kids. Mom, Aunt Faye and Carl conversed in the living room while drinking their brown whiskey, as I called it. Later that evening, Carl and Aunt Faye fell asleep on the living room sofa. We kids all shared a bedroom with Mom. After we had all gone to bed, I was briefly awakened by Carl as he lifted up a mattress on the bed where I was sleeping. Thinking nothing, I turned over and went right back to sleep. The next morning, Mom woke me asking if I had been under the mattress and taken any money. I explained that I had not done so but was briefly awakened when Carl lifted up the mattress. She stated, "Dammit, that damn Carl done clipped me!" The term, "clip" was a popular term used to describe the theft of money from someone as opposed to actually robbing someone or forcibly taking their money.

I remember thinking how lowdown and dirty that Carl had to have been in order to see Mom struggling with five small children, and still have the nerve to take her only means of income for the entire month. I was extra hard on myself for being so sleepy that I didn't realize Carl was robbing us. All I had to do was wake Mom or Aunt Faye to alert them to what was going on, but I had no idea what was happening. In fact, I was only awakened for a couple of seconds. Mom and Aunt Faye, however, had been drinking heavily along with Carl, and had been in such deep sleep that they could not have known that Carl was robbing us.

After Mom told Aunt Faye about being clipped by Carl, Aunt Faye said she would do some checking to confirm the theft. Sure enough, later that day, Aunt Faye saw Carl with a new car. She told Mom that she confronted Carl about the theft, but he denied it. Although there were no eyewitnesses to the theft, I was awakened by him lifting the mattress. We thought that was circumstantial enough. Mom filed criminal charges against Carl, but just like the situation with Dad's murder, we didn't expect to ever hear anything about it. Sure enough, we never heard anything.

Carl's theft of our monthly income had far-reaching impacts that he probably could never realize. I could not imagine someone being that low and dirty by taking our only means of survival for that month. If ever I lost faith and trust in humanity as a kid, it was then. I was so angry that I wished I could have found a gun or knife and killed him. What kind of person would commit that type of crime against a helpless family? Having been down that road before, Mom knew the landlord would not be forgiving if we did not pay the rent on time for that month. Reflecting back on the previous ouster and the dreadful and painful feeling I experienced, I asked Mom whether we would be put out on the streets again. She told me she had a few days to find some funds or another house because we for sure would get "sat out" if she could not come up with the funds. As it turned out, Mom and Aunt Faye ended up borrowing enough money to move to another house before the landlord could have a chance to kick us out of the apartment. I remember thinking what a treat that we had escaped another eviction and would be getting away from the apartments where we were constantly harassed and made to feel like animals by our own playmates. One of Mom's friends brought his pickup truck over late one night, loaded all of us inside it, along with as much of our meager belongings as he could get and drove us to our new home.

    The new house we moved into was an old rickety, wooden duplex. It was not too far from the apartments we had just left, and luckily, it was back into the Lorah Park school zone, which meant Renee and I did not have to change schools. The owner of the house was an old white man who lived next door. We affectionately called him Pop.

    Until that move, I had never been around or dealt with white people. Our world was completely black. All of our teachers were black, all of the students were black, and the owners of the small businesses we patronized were all black. Naturally, none of us knew what to think of Pop. As it turned out, he was very good to us. In fact, we deemed him our savior for that time period, and we were very grateful for him. Whenever Mom was short on funds, Pop would loan her a few dollars, and would sometimes let her pay rent a few days later. During that time, Aunt Faye stayed with us, and she even did regular house cleaning for Pop. After a while, it seemed like Pop had essentially become a part of the family. Oftentimes, Mom would prepare him a plate of whatever she cooked for dinner, and since Pop drank liquor, it was not uncommon to find him at our side of the duplex drinking beer or liquor with Mom and Aunt Faye.

Attending three schools within one school year was really starting to take its toll on me. It was hard enough being the new kid at school once a year, but three times in one year was a bit much to endure. I'm sure the other kids sensed Renee and my intimidation level because they taunted us about our clothes, bullied us, and on several occasions, physically struck us during our walk home from school. I never liked fighting, but would do so only as a means of survival, which was frequently the case during those days, but I was no match against a large group of kids. So, I had to choose wisely whether to swing fists or retreat. I recall on one instance, this girl named Gail grabbed my shirt so hard that the whole thing just tore apart which caused me to literally walk home without a shirt. I couldn't retaliate because her brother, cousin, and a few other friends would have seriously gang-beat me well beyond the level of harassment they were already administering at the time. So, against my strong desire to retaliate, I endured the taunts and light slaps to my head for the rest of the walk home. After that day, Renee and I started taking the long way to and from school, even though it added substantially more distance and time to our regular route, which was already about a mile long. The peace of mind and freedom from harassment, however, was well worth the extra effort.

Finally, that roller coaster school year ended, and summer was a welcomed relief from the hell I caught during the school year. I struggled in every school subject except reading and I had no friends. Aunt Faye was no longer working as a live-in housekeeper, and as a result, we no longer received the nice hand-me-downs from Jewish children as they grew older. That meant I was always wearing old, ragged, or dirty clothes, which caused other children to poke fun at me. The one thing I really missed about school were the free lunches that I received daily, as the summers were always pretty rough regarding food.

While at home that summer, I noticed Mom and Aunt Faye constantly had visitors to the house, and on many occasions, they drank a lot of beer. That constant presence of beer is what really started me drinking. I knew the dangers of drinking and stayed away from liquor due to the drinking accident that almost killed me years prior, although at age eight, I could easily get it if I desired to do so. Instead, I focused on beer. Whenever the adults would leave unfinished cans of beer around, I'd sneak and take a quick drink from the can, and before too long, I started taking several drinks, which then led to me just swiping entire 16-ounce cans of the beer and going out on the back porch to sip drinks while no one was watching.

During one of my trips to the back porch to sip on a can of beer that was left unattended, I was alarmed by the sound of screaming coming from inside the house. As I ran inside, I saw that the curtains to one of our windows was on fire. My sister Renee was upset because she uttered some curse words and Aunt Faye gave her a few swats with a belt. In response, Renee picked up a book of matches, and set fire to one of the plastic curtains that hung at the window. The thin plastic material quickly burned, and were it not for Aunt Faye's quick action, the old wooden house may have burned down. Fortunately, other than charred wood around the window, the fire didn't cause any other damage. That window was never repaired and remained in the same condition until we moved away from the house.

We didn't live in Pop's duplex for very long. On several occasions, I overheard him telling Mom and Aunt Faye that his grown children wanted to take him away to live with another relative because they wanted both sides of the duplex for themselves. Because he always seemed to give Mom and Aunt Faye small bits of information at a time, they never were sure he was telling them everything. Finally, Pop convinced them that his children were not telling him everything he needed to know, because they feared he would share it with

Mom and Aunt Faye. Finally, one afternoon, the one thing we all feared came to fruition—Pop's son pulled up in his car and without saying anything to me as I sat on the porch, went directly into Pop's side of the duplex. Sensing something was wrong, I rushed into the house to tell Mom and Aunt Faye what I had seen and felt. In response, they rushed out to the front porch. Within a few minutes, Pop's son exited the house and placed some of Pop's items in the car. As he returned to the house, he looked at Mom, and stated, "My dad's going to live with a family member. It's time for you folks to find another place to live."

Upon receiving the verbal eviction order, Mom and Aunt Faye erupted into an episode of cursing that I had never heard beforehand! Both sisters were experts at cursing, but Aunt Faye was the most notorious curser I had ever seen. They both hit the son with so many curse words, that all he could do was stand there and look at them with an odd grin. He then spoke up and said, "I'm sorry, you folks must leave by next Friday, or I will have you arrested for trespassing." During the son's next trip to the car, Pop exited the house with him. He sadly looked at Mom and Aunt Faye and said "Girls, I'm not well and I have to go live with a daughter I hate. My son is gonna be taking over the duplex, but I begged him to give y'all some time before kicking you out. He agreed to give you a week to find another place." Mom and Aunt Faye hugged Pop as he got into his son's car that quickly sped away. After they drove off, Mom said "Well I'll be damned! I got to go out and find another place to live!

Chapter 9

Poison

As a result of all of the moving, I continued to struggle academically. Reading was no problem because I always had an interest in reading and I didn't encounter too many problems with that subject. We never had books in our house, so I would read whatever I could get my hands on. Usually, that was the back of a detergent box or house cleaner container. I would read directions, the hazard statements, and even the chemical make-up of the products. Or sometimes, people would leave old newspapers or magazines at the public laundry mat. I would collect them, take them back home and read them with great interest.

Education was not an enormous issue in our home, but somehow, I always felt there was some type of magnet pulling me toward books and reading. Other than reading, everything else was just a blur. Math and science were the worst. While all of the other kids seemed to master basic multiplication tables and science principles, I was stuck trying to understand the tricks to such mastery. But another summer had arrived and I decided I'd worry about my deficiencies when school began in the fall.

Late one evening after Mom got her social security checks and went to cash them, the previous year's horror that I thought would never be repeated was in fact repeated. She came inside the house frantically sobbing while telling me that a man had snatched her purse again. I literally couldn't believe what I was hearing. The horrifying thought and humiliation of being "put out" on the streets, of having no food, and of losing our belongings overcame me that very moment. I felt like I needed to do something, but at the same time, I felt completely helpless. That was the same feeling I had experienced when I stood looking at Dad's slain body, as well as when Mom was robbed the first time. At least this time I knew what to expect, and sure enough, within two weeks' time, our belongings were forcibly removed from the house and placed outside on the sidewalk. We were kicked out again.

Mom had a few days to prepare for the eviction, and although we stayed with a friend of hers for a few days, we were able to quickly get into another house. The house was near NW 62nd Street, and not far from Gladeview Elementary School, which would become our new school.

It was during that most recent ouster that a nagging thought became more prominent. Poison! Many times while reading the back of cleaning product containers, I would read that the items were poisonous and harmful if swallowed. Based on my reading, I knew I couldn't let the products touch my skin, and that if any got into my eyes, I needed to flush them with water, or if any were swallowed, I needed to vomit. I knew I was dealing with some seriously harmful substances, and I also knew I could end my misery if I mixed the products with water and drank the mixture.

One day, shortly after moving to the new house, I decided to go for it, and drink a poisonous drink that would kill me. It was one of the most terrifying decisions I had to make. As I pondered how I would carry out my plan, my mind thought back to a few years earlier when my brother Darrell fell to the floor while we children were home alone, and laid there in what appeared to be a tranced state for several minutes until he defecated in his underpants. We children just stood around looking at him but had absolutely no idea what to do. Once he finished, I cleaned him up, and he got up and resumed his normal activity. I had never seen anything as weird as what happened to Darrell; nor could I adequately explain it. When Mom got home from work, all we could explain was that Darrell died earlier that day, but came back to life after he "boo-booed" in his clothes. Mom couldn't understand what we were trying to explain, and as such, she didn't appear to associate much seriousness with our claims, which meant she did not take Darrell to the hospital or anything. I always thought Darrell would experience that weird episode again due to Mom not seeking medical attention, but fortunately, nothing ever happened again.

After reliving Darrell's episode over and over in my mind, I thought how lucky I would be if I didn't have to live the life we were living. I was always so sad and resentful about everything. I was barely ten years old and couldn't even recall when I was a child. All I could remember were the adult-like responsibilities that I had to carry out each day. My older sister Janice was still in Georgia with Grandma, and since I was the oldest child at home, everything fell upon me. Within a few short years, I had literally transitioned from a child happily riding in Dad's big diesel truck, to one with adult-like responsibilities although I had not even reached puberty. The burden of taking care of my family was just too great and had really started taking its toll on me.

Finally, I talked myself into making the drink that would take me out. Although I didn't know for sure, I always suspected that Darrell experienced that temporary "death" years earlier because he drank one of the poisonous cleaning fluids from the bathroom cabinet that I frequently read about. I also thought about the fifth of vodka that took me out a few years earlier, and finally, I thought about me giving my sister Renee some bleach to drink when we were very young. I told her it was water, and when she took a drink, she immediately spit it out and vomited. I enjoyed the gag trick that I played, but Mom was not amused and beat me pretty bad that day, while saying that I could have killed Renee with such a stupid trick.

Since I had a good idea of what would kill me, I mixed pine cleaner, bleach, detergent and ammonia into a cup with water and stirred it for what seemed like forever. I wasn't sure if the lengthy stirring was a delay tactic on my behalf, or whether I was trying to get the concoction as fine as I could in order to make it go down as smoothly as possible. Whatever the case, I stirred for at least five minutes. Then, as the moment of reckoning arrived, I put the drink to my nose for a smell test. It was so strong that I lost my breath for a second. Then, the doubts started. I thought what if it didn't work? Still, my situation was so dire that I wanted to get it over.

For a second, I thought maybe I shouldn't drink the concoction, and instead, eat some of the rat poison that we placed in cabinets in our futile efforts to kill off our rat infestation, but then I thought if the rat poison would not kill the rats, it would be completely harmless to me. I then figured I had run out of time, and that I had to drink the poison at that very moment. So, I took a sip, and wow, what an experience!

The combined taste and smell brought about an immediate reflux, and instead of going down, the liquid burst forward out of my mouth on the bathroom mirror, as I leaned over the sink coughing while trying to catch my breath! I tried to vomit, but I couldn't make anything come up. All I could think of was to put as much water in my mouth and rinse every bit of the poison out.

After about five minutes of mouth rinsing, I still had the worst taste in my mouth that I had ever known. I rubbed toothpaste on my irritated tongue, but it did nothing to relieve the pain or the taste.

Finally, I looked in the refrigerator, and found a half-eaten dill pickle. The sour taste helped a tad bit, but I just could not seem to get rid of the irritation. After a couple of days, my mouth and tongue appeared to get back to normal, and since everything seemed okay, I didn't tell Mom anything about my failed attempt to kill myself.

Chapter 10

Mr. Crews

Being ousted from Pop's place meant Renee and I had to endure yet another school change for the new school year. Since we had most of the summer to mentally prepare for our new school, Gladeview Elementary, we didn't feel as intimidated as we felt whenever we had to transfer schools in the middle of the school year.

On the first day of school at Gladeview, something told me that would be a special place. On that day, I encountered the first role model of my life, after the death of my father. He was my 5th grade teacher, Mr. Daniel Crews, a tall, thin, brown-skinned black man. As far as I was concerned, Mr. Crews was my new father. Other than my own dad, I had never really had close dealings with adult men. All of my teachers had been black women. Mom and Aunt Faye had men friends who came to the house, but I had no real dealings with them. We had lost contact with my dad's brothers after Dad died, and since we did not have the luxury of a telephone, it was almost impossible for any relatives to keep up with us due to our frequent moves. So, Mr. Crews was my guy. I looked forward to going to school every day, and I did my very best because I wanted to always stand out to him. I remember, he once asked me to go to his car to retrieve something. When I got to the car, I just stood there awestruck as I admired this beautiful, shiny Cadillac. Just his asking me to run that errand landed me on the moon. In that one instant, all the hurt, loneliness, despair and grief I privately endured over the past few years since Dad's death just sort of evaporated. For once in my life since Dad's death, a sense of happiness crept into my mind.

At age 10, I was a very private person. Mom had always taught us to keep our business inside the house. But I felt like Mr. Crews knew me and my family's plight. He would always ask me how things were going, and I'd always say, "Okay," but his looks always told me that he knew the hell I was catching. He would always tell me he knew I was going to be something special one day. I never could understand what he meant, but in response, I'd always flash the biggest smile possible, because it felt good that somebody was telling me something of such a positive nature.

I wasn't alone. All of the class loved Mr. Crews. Our all-black class was a mixture of fifth and sixth grade students of varying abilities, but despite that, Mr. Crews was able to effectively teach all of us. Only two of us fifth graders could not grasp multiplication tables, but Mr. Crews kept working with us, while telling us he was not going to allow any of his students to leave fifth grade without knowing the one through twelve multiplication tables. Over time, we both finally figured out how to memorize the tables and were then able to catch up with the other fifth graders. It was such an accomplishment for me, but it seemed like an even bigger accomplishment for Mr. Crews. I loved Mr. Crews to no end, because for once in my life, I knew somebody believed in me.

Mr. Crews showed his best side when he saved me from what would have been an extremely humiliating experience. Our class was preparing for the school's annual end of the year class play and had spent many weeks rehearsing under Mr. Crews' direction. We were also getting nearer to the time where we had to do full dress rehearsals in the outfits that our parents were supposed to have purchased for us. That year's play was centered around a lot of the music of that era, and our outfits were supposed to represent such. We were singing the 5th Dimensions' songs, "Age of Aquarius" and "Let the Sunshine In," as well as the Temptations' songs "Psychedelic Shack" and "I Can't Get Next To You." Groovy outfits were the norm. We were all expected to wear vests with fringes and beads, bell bottoms, and psychedelic clothing. Although we called the event a play, it was more like a talent show.

As I visualized how we would look, and what I would wear for the play, I slowly came to the realization that at home, we could barely pay for rent and other necessities, and Mom could not afford to buy special outfits for me to be in a school play. So, I did not even waste time to talk to her about the money. Instead, I approached Mr. Crews and told him Mom said I could not be in the play because she could not afford the cost. He suggested that Mom indicate how much she could pay, and he would pay the rest. I thought to myself,

"We can't pay any of it," but, instead of saying anything right then, I waited until the next day to tell him that Mom said she could not pay any of it, although I had not spoken to Mom at all about the issue. Mr. Crews then worked out a perfect solution. He told the class he was excited about the play, but unfortunately, he was going to need someone to give up their part and assist with the audio-visual equipment, and that he would give some extra credit for doing such. He then looked around the room and stopped at me, and said, "Cecil, can you do it?" Of course, I jumped at the opportunity as I knew he had specially carved that job out for me as a way to make me look good in the face of a potentially embarrassing situation.

The school play was carried out perfectly. Each of my classmates participated, and each wore the exact outfits they were told they needed to wear. I marveled that each of their parents could afford their outfits, while I was the only one in such a dire situation. I didn't fret too long because I had an important job to do to make sure the music came on when it was supposed to do so. When the play ended and my class members took their respective bows, Mr. Crews directed the audience attention to me, and mentioned that I had one of the most important parts in the play, and that if the music did not come on when needed, things would have gone badly. I will never forget how special I felt as Mr. Crews talked about me. He took a potentially horrid situation and created gold. I walked on air the rest of the day.

As the school year ended, I was elated to know that the fifth graders in Mr. Crews' fifth/sixth grade class would return to his class for sixth grade. I didn't even look forward to the long summer. I loved school too much, and I loved Mr. Crews even more. Unbeknownst to him, he allowed me to dream and escape from my world of fear and poverty. Being around him definitely motivated me and changed my outlook on life. When I looked back, the best way I could explain Mr. Crews' impact on me, was he stopped the suffocating. He was the oxygen a young, angry, confused, and wayward kid like me needed in order to sustain life. Life, up until that point, had been so full of hurt and disappointment, but somehow, I sensed that Mr. Crews knew that and did all he could to help ease the pain. I don't know if Mr. Crews had any special gifts or anything, but I do feel absolutely certain, he was sent by God to Gladeview Elementary to teach the combined fifth/sixth grade class that I would be a part of. His presence alone was enough to keep me on a straight path, but his intuition drove his actions, and his actions impacted me in a way that made me believe I was smart, intelligent, and not just a throw away piece of trash. He was the best dad a fatherless kid could ever have.

Chapter 11

A Lesson Learned

With school out for the summer, eating a regular meal on a regular basis was somewhat of a challenge. The beginning of the month was fine because Mom's checks would come in and later in the month, she would make her regular trip to the welfare office in order to get food. But, as the end of the month drew near, food became scarce. Fortunately, fruit such as mangoes, cherries, guavas, Chinese plums, sea grapes, and coconuts grew wild in Miami, so there was always something fresh and healthy to snack on. But, from time to time, we needed more than just tropical fruits, but more was not available.

One day, unbeknownst to Mom, I went to Ralph's Super Market to pick up a pack of bologna, which we referred to as baloney. The only problem is I did not have money with me. As I selected a nice sized package that contained many slices of baloney, I slipped it into the front of my pants thinking my shirt would conceal it from anyone who became suspicious of what was going on. I didn't anticipate how cold the package would feel against my underbody, but once I hid it, I could not risk repositioning it. So, I walked toward the exit in a very awkward manner, but before I could get to the exit, a very large and intimidating black man came behind me, grabbed me by the arm and said in the most intimidating voice I had ever heard, "Come with me!"

All of a sudden that package of baloney didn't feel so cold anymore. My entire body flashed hot as if someone had just lit a fire inside me. The security guy had on what looked to be a police uniform, and that's what I associated him with. I just knew I was going to jail for life. Interestingly, instead of taking me directly to the back of the store where I thought he would take me, he instead took me to a belt rack and told me to "Pick one!" In those days, the supermarket carried items other than food. They also carried clothing and household items. In fact, oftentimes, Mom purchased our school sneakers from the supermarket.

I could not understand why the big black guy was telling me to pick out a belt, so initially I resisted, probably because I was just too horrified to comprehend what was going on. Eventually, he said he was going to give me a beating, and that I better pick out a belt before he picked one out for me.

As a kid, I was no stranger to getting beatings with belts, and I always subscribed to a theory that it was better to get a beating with a wide and thick belt as opposed to a skinny belt because the skinny belt stung worse than the thick belt. So, I picked out the widest belt they had and handed it to the big guy. He then took me to a small office near the back of the store behind several stacks of boxes. He then asked me what the hell did I think I was doing, and where did I live? By then, my eyes had gotten watery, but I was not fully crying. I was also trembling with the type fear I had not experienced since Hurricane Cleo.

Usually, I could always talk myself out of most situations, so I begged the big black guy not to beat me and promised him that I would never come into the store again. My efforts to persuade him, however, did not work. He replied in that booming voice, "You a lie! I'm gonna teach you not to steal from me again!" I replied, "I didn't steal from you, I was gonna come back and pay for it!" I'm not sure what cell inside my body made me utter that response to this man, but based on his facial expression, I could tell something set him off. He then grabbed me and literally threw me onto a desk and placed one hand on my back to hold me down and gave me a hard swat to my butt with that wide belt. I screamed and started crying loudly, thinking someone would hear me and come to rescue me. I continually pleaded with him that I would never steal again if he would let me go.

While I was holding tight to my butt, crying, and screaming for him to please don't hit me again, he just stood there and watched me. I instantly felt I was getting to him, and that he was sensing my sincerity. So, I continued my act. After another minute or so, the big black guy sat down and told me to sit down. He peered straight into my eyes with a look I had never gotten from anyone, and said, "Look little Negro, you seem like a good kid, and I don't want you to end up in prison for the rest of your life, so if I don't whip your lil butt anymore, do you promise not to ever commit another crime in your life again?"

Sensing that the beating was probably coming to an end, I quickly promised that he would never have to deal with me again. At that point, he uttered a statement that Mom had often said. He said, "I'm only doing this because I love you, and if I didn't love you, I wouldn't be doing this." As a kid, my quiet response was always, "Please hate me" because I hated getting beatings. When he released me, I quickly got out of the store without looking back.

The rest of that summer, I must have passed Ralph's Super Market a thousand times, but never would I go inside again. The big black dude placed a measure of fear in me that was sufficient to last a lifetime. I even passed up opportunities to go inside when I was with Mom. The experience was just too traumatic. Plus, Mom never knew what happened, and the last thing I needed was the big black dude spilling the beans.

The fallout from my encounter with the big black guy was my "buggy hustling" job at Ralph's. On Fridays, Saturdays, and Sundays, several boys around my age would line up outside the grocery store doors, and one-by-one, we would assist customers with placing their groceries into their cars. They gave us tips ranging from a quarter to a dollar bill. It was a great way to earn spending money, and money to help Mom with food costs.

After my encounter, I never went back. I wasn't sure if it was fear, embarrassment, shame, or even pride, but I had decided I would never step foot in or at that store again, and that's what I did. The big black dude did not ban me from the store. In fact, he probably would have enjoyed seeing me change, but I just could not make myself go inside again. That man's single act affected my life in a major way. I am a living tribute to him.

Chapter 12

Uncle John

One day, a strange man appeared at our door, as Mom delightfully screamed his name and hugged him. She introduced him to us as her brother John. He had just arrived in Miami from Georgia. Uncle John stayed with us for a short period of time and then we saw him no more. Then he started a very consistent pattern. He would come to see us for a day or so, help cook, and then disappear. His fried green tomatoes were the absolute best eating of my childhood. As best we kids could understand, Uncle John lived on the streets. He was basically homeless. Mom always said he knew he had a place to lay his head if he needed to do so, but he preferred to "live in the streets."

Aunt Faye, in her very own special way just told us that Uncle John was a hobo. That's the first time I heard that word. She explained that Uncle John never stayed in one place long, and that he drank nothing but wine, and lived wherever he could. I remember him always having a pungent smell about himself, and his breath always smelled as if he had in fact, just finished drinking a bottle of wine. Every time Uncle John visited, Mom would try to get him to stay, but after a good dinner, a much-needed bath, and a batch of fried green tomatoes, he would be leave again.

The second time in my life when I experienced the death of a close family member was when Uncle John died. Mom and Aunt Faye were extremely upset to find out that their only brother had been found dead in the very spot behind a store where he and several other homeless men hung out. The only explanation Mom gave me was that John drank himself to death. I knew Uncle John drank a lot of wine, and you could smell it on his breath whenever he was near, but I did not know a person could die as a result.

I don't know if an official cause of death was ever given other than the reasons given to me. We did not have a telephone, but Mom was able to get in touch with her mother and sisters in Georgia by way of Western Union, which was the preferred mode of communication for many people in our community during that time.

Then late one night, Mom awakened all of us to meet our Grandma OnaBell, and other aunts for the first time that I could recall. They had just arrived after a long trip from Quitman, Georgia to Miami for Uncle John's funeral. Grandma OnaBell, along with three other aunts and a cousin made the trip. They all knew Renee and me because we were born in Georgia, but we did not know them, as we had not seen them since we were toddlers. Dad had taken us back to Georgia a couple of times, but we only visited his mother, Grandma Susie Lee. For some reason, we never saw Grandma OnaBell.

After the funeral, Mom made one of the smartest decisions of her life. She sent Renee back to live with Grandma OnaBell. My oldest sister Janice had been in Georgia for years, first with Grandma Susie Lee, and then with Grandma OnaBell. So, Renee would finally be with her big sister, while the four boys stayed in Miami.

I missed Uncle John's visits and his fried green tomatoes that he would cook whenever he came over. The only other male family member I really knew was no longer alive.

Chapter 13

Adolescence

By the time summer started, Mom had started dating some guy named Jake. I did not think much of him, and I did not think he would be around for too long. Plus, he drank heavily, and although Mom was a regular beer drinker, she started heavily drinking liquor as well. Before too long, Jake had moved in with us, and within a couple of weeks, one of his sons, Craig, who was about three years older than me, moved in. I had become accustomed to being the man of the house. By then, I could cook decently, I could clean house, I could help my brothers with homework in the form of "playing school," and I could push a shopping cart full of dirty clothes to the laundry mat about a half mile from the house and wash and dry several loads of clothes. So, I did not feel the need for other strangers in the house. But they were there, and I figured I would make the best of the situation. Plus, it was cool to have a big brother of sorts.

Jake and Craig had not been with us long before a familiar foe reared its head again—the Sheriff's movers. For the third time, our house was involuntarily pad locked and our belongings were put out on the street. This time, we all stood by and watched two burly white men move everything out. The humiliation was great, as neighbors stood by and pitifully watched, as if they knew it could have just as easily been them. The sting of that latest eviction only worsened after a hard rain drenched our load of belongings and essentially turned them into what resembled a load of rubbish.

Where was Mr. Crews when I needed him most? I did not know whether I was more hurt or embarrassed by this happening of events. That familiar feeling of helplessness overcame me again and all I could think of was where could I escape? If I had known where Mr. Crews lived, I would have walked directly to his home to let my emotions go, no matter how far away he lived. Since Gladeview was not too far from us, I walked to the school thinking someone might be there to tell me how to get in touch with Mr. Crews. To my dismay, I could not find a single person. The school was closed that summer afternoon.

During my walk back to the house, I kept asking myself, why me? I couldn't understand how a kid who was about to turn eleven years old was having such a hard time. Nobody else my age seemed to be in a similar situation. The only person in the world I thought would understand me was Mr. Crews, but I could not locate him. I was so desperate that as I walked past Ralph's Super Market, I almost walked inside to look for the big black guy. He brutalized me, but at the same time told me he did it because he loved me. Maybe he would understand my pain and dismay and tell me to hang in there or something. But, my inner sense of not placing my hand on a hot stove a second time prevailed. That man struck some serious fear and pain in me that I will never forget.

By the time I returned to the house, Jake had come home. He had a sister named Mavis who lived about a half mile or so from us. He told us to recoup whatever clothing we could from the wet pile, and packed us into his old dusty blue Plymouth, and took us to Mavis's house. I knew Mavis, as she had visited our house a few times, when she and Mom went out on the town. She was a bit larger than Mom and wore a girdle when she dressed up such that it made that "squish-squish" sound that girdles tend to make. I liked her and found a sense of relief when I discovered we were going to her house. Craig had often fondly talked about Mavis's children, his cousins, so I felt I knew them before ever meeting them.

When we arrived at Mavis's house four streets away, we found a large white wooden house with a wrap-around porch. It was the nicest house we had ever lived in. The house needed to be big, because Mavis's family was enormous! She and her husband Arthur lived there along with nine children. The children were all ages from toddler to adult. Now, added to that mix was Mom, Jake, Craig, myself and my three younger brothers. The house literally slept sixteen of us, and to add to that, Mavis's daughter Annie was pregnant, and gave birth to a son that summer.

Living in close quarters with Mavis's family was not the most comfortable feeling in the world, but it sure beat having your belongings thrown outside onto the street! After a few weeks, Aunt Faye came to visit us. Since we did not have phones, I'm not sure how she found us, but she did. After her visit, she agreed to let me go home with her. She had a nice one-bedroom apartment across town in the Overtown section of Miami where we had previously lived. Initially, being in Overtown brought back sad memories of Dad being slain, and of being kicked out of our apartment, but after a few days, I settled down, and for the first time since Dad died, I actually relaxed.

After being in Overtown for a few days, I actually started liking it. Aunt Faye lived near busy NW 2nd Avenue that was always bustling with people as a result of the many stores, bars, pool halls, drug stores, churches, and restaurants. Sometimes, I would just sit at the door of a bar and watch the patrons dance and enjoy themselves. Every now and then, someone would run me away, but typically, everybody minded their own business and nobody bothered me. I could sit there for hours listening to the sounds of James Brown, Stevie Wonder, and Aretha Franklin blaring out onto the sidewalks, and watch passersby stop and do a few dances in front of the bar before continuing their walk. That particular trip to Overtown solidified my love for soul music. It got to the point that I knew every word to every song that was played on the jukebox, and sometimes, I would even dance on the sidewalks in front of the bar the music was coming from. The music definitely had a magnetic effect on me. If a song was playing, chances are I was right outside the bar singing along. Many of the adults started recognizing me, and knew I was Aunt Faye's nephew, so they did not bother me too much. I don't recall too many other kids hanging around the bars, but those who did, tended to not harass me.

One morning after Aunt Faye had gone to her cleaning job at a hotel near downtown Miami, I got up and cleaned the apartment, then opened all the blinds and windows to let the sun shine in. Immediately, I heard Stevie Wonder's hit song, "Signed, Sealed, Delivered," blaring from one of the bars' jukebox below. I remember thinking I would never forget that one brief moment of peace and calm. To this very day, whenever I hear that song, my heart and mind goes back to the summer of 1970 when I felt a slither of happiness and peace. Despite everything else that was going on or had gone on, for that one brief moment in time, everything just went away as I gazed out the window below, while my thoughts floated a million miles away.

The rest of that summer was pretty uneventful by our standards. One of Mavis's sons, Donny was a year younger than me, so we bonded pretty close and spent the summer doing what boys our age did. Slowly, I was realizing that I did not have all of the major responsibilities I previously had. That summer gave Donny and me time to engage in our favorite pastime of throwing rocks at cars, stealing mangoes from neighbors' yards, collecting and selling used soda bottles for five cents each, and getting into whatever other mischief we could find.

That summer was also the summer of exploring interest

in girls, although my first attempt at exploration resulted in a pretty severe beating. Rose and her family lived two doors down from Mavis, and her cousin Diane was visiting for the summer from Chicago. Diane was about a year or so older than me but was much taller. One day while we were all standing around softly sizing each other up, a mischievous nerve flared up, and without warning or permission, I reached out and grabbed Diane's breasts. She quickly grabbed me, threw me to the ground, and came at me with the fierceness of a hungry tiger! After realizing the imminent danger, I quickly jumped to my feet and ran for dear life with Diane hot on my trails, knowing that if she caught me, she would beat me to a pulp. Although Diane did not catch me that day, she vowed to beat me stupid when she got her hands on me. So, for the next few days, I would not walk past Rose's house, regardless of whether I was alone or with others. Instead, I would go across the street, and walk behind the neighbors' houses until I was out of the danger zone.

Diane would see me making my detours but knew she could never catch me if she chased me. Her only hope was that I would face her like a man. While I did not want to take the chance of facing Diane, I found it quite amusing to constantly tease and heckle her, thus making her angrier with me, but completely oblivious to the fact that I was making my own situation much worse.

Then, the day of reckoning finally came. I got tired of having to go out of the way to avoid Diane. I figured I would walk straight down the street, face her, and deal with whatever happened. Although she was bigger, I foolishly rationalized that I could save face if we fought and the fight ended in a tie, or better yet, if someone stopped it before things got too bad. Unfortunately, neither happened. As I walked past Rose's house, Diane came out to greet me as if she could not believe I was actually there. I'm sure she wondered what she had done to deserve having a gift dropped right into her hands. I was intimidated but could not show it. I needed her to have second thoughts and just back off and say I was not worth the effort. That was not going to happen though.

When Diane got within an arm's reach of me, that was the end. She grabbed me and despite the pitiful effort I put forth, my world literally turned upside down! I felt like I was involved in one of those cartoon fights where you only see hands, feet, stars, and a ton of dust. That girl took out an entire summer's worth of frustration on me in the process of beating me to a pulp. It's likely she picked me up by one arm and one leg and spun me around like a helicopter, while sweeping the street with my body, but I could not tell because things were happening way too fast.

When that woodshed type whooping was finally over, my elbows and knees were scraped and I looked as if I had been dragged through the streets. Additionally, one side of my face was so severely scratched that Mom thought an animal had attacked me. I felt like I had actually been attacked by an animal. One good thing came out of the whooping that Diane gave me – I no longer had to avoid her. I could then walk past Rose's house without worrying if Diane would come out and catch me. I endured the humiliation of that beat down for quite a long time. Needless to say, I was glad to see Diane go home that summer.

Chapter 14

Integration

By the time summer ended, Mom had found us a house one street over from Mavis's house. It was a small 2-bedroom wooden house with holes in the floor where we could see the ground, but it was home to us. It was also home to a ton of rats and roaches, and although we set many rat traps and other creative efforts to limit our rodent population, we were never successful in getting rid of them. We actually learned to coexist with them by not leaving food out, and by cleaning up after eating.

Fortunately, none of us ever got attacked by any of the rodents, but we constantly encountered huge roaches in our kitchen cabinets and drawers. We learned then, that the best way to cope in addition to not leaving food out was to rinse every plate and utensil before using them even if they were already cleaned. That practice stayed with me forever. Even when I went to other people's houses, I would rinse a utensil or a cup if I had to take one from the drawer. I did not intend my actions as an insult to the hosts; it was just a practice I had become accustomed to as a result of my own situation.

Based on our latest move, I was devastated to learn I would not be going back to Gladeview for sixth grade with Mr. Crews. The first thought I had was that I was being rejected again, and that every time something appeared to move forward, something came out of nowhere to push it backward. I suspected I would not be going back because our house was on 56th Street, which was too far south to be included in Gladeview's zone. We would have needed to be four blocks north on 60th Street. I just figured Mom would do what she had done once before, and not actually do the transfer. The extra walk to school would have definitely been worth it for me to have the fatherly mentorship of Mr. Crews for another year.

To my surprise, Mom conducted the transfer and the consolation I received was that I would be going back to Lorah Park, the same school I had attended two years previously. There was a tad bit of relief in knowing that for once, I was not going to a new school. At least I would know many of the students who were there in third and part of fourth grade with me. Plus, having spent the summer in the neighborhood, I had met many kids who I would be going to school with. What I did not know, however, was that the school board had decided to integrate the public schools and would be implementing a busing plan before school started. All 5th and 6th graders in my zone who should have been reporting to Lorah Park were to be bussed a couple of miles away to the City of Miami Springs, to attend all-white Glenn Curtis Elementary.

The busing experiment was weird for all of us. None of the kids from my completely segregated Brown Sub neighborhood had gone to school with white or Cuban kids and the white and Cuban kids from Miami Springs had probably never gone to school with black kids. I suppose the county's integration plan did not include movement of teachers, because we black kids had experienced all black teachers up to that point, and when we got to Glenn Curtis, we discovered that all their teachers were white. So, for the first time in my life, I had a white teacher.

Despite the major change, we did not have many problems. In fact, it seemed as though we had less fights at Glenn Curtis than we had at our schools in Brown Sub. There were small instances of what I perceived as racism, but by and large, we made it through the year okay.

In one instance, a white student named Paul came up to me with a world map in his hand. His finger was pointed to the country, Niger, as he very seriously asked me how to pronounce it. I seriously pondered for a moment, trying to remember rules of pronunciation before explaining to him that the name of the country rhymed with tiger, except the "g" had the "j" sound. I then correctly pronounced it for him.

Paul very seriously said, "Oh, okay, I see," as he went along his business. As he walked away, I shook my head, saying he knew where he was trying to go with that word. I concluded that he wanted me to say the name of the country was Nigger, but I was not going there with him.

Another instance happened outside during physical

education. I had a basketball to myself, just lazily shooting it through the hoop, and was not in a mood to play with anyone. Out of nowhere, two white classmates, Tim and Roger, came behind me, stole the ball, and refused to give it back. When I went to one, he would throw it to the other, and this was repeated over and over until I picked up a rock and dared Roger to throw it again. When he threw it back to Tim, I threw the rock and hit him. They reported me to Mr. Patterson, our white teacher, and he reported me to the principal who gave me a paddling. Tim and Roger, however, got no punishment despite being the agitators.

    I sensed extreme unfairness with how the rock-throwing incident was handled, and Mom's response did not make me feel any better. She always took the position that once we went to school, we were under the direction and control of the school officials, and whatever they did or said was always right. There were many instances where I felt something was done wrong to me or my siblings at school, and mom would have the same response. As I dealt with schools on my children's behalf, I finally realized how intimidated Mom had to have been with the officials at our schools, especially those at the integrated schools. I then realized why she never questioned their actions, despite how wrong or unfair they may have been.

    As the school year drew near the end, the conversation about which middle schools (or junior high, as we called them) we would attend the following year became a major topic. After having gone to six schools in six years, that topic was not a huge issue for me. At least I would be attending a different school as a part of a natural transition, and not because we were forced to change our living arrangement at the spur of the moment. I was told I would be going to Charles Drew Jr. High, and was most upset because the other kids in the neighborhood would be attending Brownsville Jr. High.

What I discovered later was that our street, 56th Street, was a major dividing line for school zones. Those living on the south side of 56th Street were assigned to Brownsville, and ultimately Jackson High School, while those on the north side of the street would go to Charles Drew, and ultimately Northwestern High School. I was not a happy camper. Charles Drew was in the heart of the Liberty City section of Miami, right near several federal government housing projects, which I wanted no part of. I wanted Brownsville Jr. High and Jackson Sr. High.

Chapter 15

Hustling

The bus ride to Glenn Curtis was only about two and a half miles from our community and took most of us out of the black community for the first time in our lives. Those rides allowed us 5th and 6th graders to realize that our community was separated from the white and Cuban community by a large warehouse and industrial district. Naturally, my exploration instincts prevailed, and on several occasions, three or four of us would intentionally miss our school bus and walk the two and a half miles home, but not before checking out what was going on at the nearby factories.

When the school year ended, my friend Albert from across the street, my younger brother Tony and I constantly sought out ways to make money. I remembered the factories that we peeked into during those walks home from school, so the three of us decided to visit them while on our mission to find money sources. Albert was a year older than me, but had an entrepreneurial spirit like me, and because I was Tony's older brother, he basically followed me in whatever I did. While hanging out around the factories, we noticed that the workers were almost all Cuban, and we knew avocados were a favorite food for Cubans. Although avocado trees grew everywhere in our neighborhood, none of us ate them. I could never acquire a taste for the fruit, even when we doctored it up with salt, pepper, vinegar, onions, or other spices believed to hide the taste.

It didn't take us long to realize the income potential from selling the avocados to the Cuban workers. Typically, two of us would climb trees to pick the avocados and toss them down to the other person on the ground. We would fill a shopping basket, or buggy, as we called it, and push it from the neighborhood to the warehouses approximately a quarter to half mile away. We had to be sure to schedule our appearance right at the time of lunch when the workers would come out to the lunch trucks. By selling the avocados at a quarter to fifty cents, depending on size, we would easily sell out an entire buggy within about thirty minutes, and make about fifteen dollars, or so. We'd split the money and make plans for the next trip.

Mango trees covered our neighborhood about as much as avocado trees, but the difference was that everybody in our neighborhood loved eating mangoes, which made it difficult to become income producers, but from time to time, we would luck up and get to a tree that produced the large succulent type of mango that was too valuable to eat. Those types of mangoes could easily command a dollar each. The small turpentine mangoes were worthless for selling, so we would eat those instead.

The problem with the large succulent mangoes was that they were usually in trees belonging to other people, which meant if we wanted them, we had to climb someone else's tree and literally steal their mangoes. Since the large mangoes could command a dollar each, we always rationalized that it was worth the risk of getting caught stealing them. Plus, we thought the most that could come out of getting caught was someone would chase us away, or maybe tell our mothers.

There was one house in our neighborhood down toward the corner heading toward the industrial district that produced some of the biggest and prettiest mangoes around. We knew someone lived in the house, but we did not know them, and we rarely saw anyone there. We kept a watchful eye on the house for a couple of days, hoping to get an idea when they left home or returned. After seeing no activity for a couple of days, we decided to pay a visit. We figured since the house was on the far corner, the chance of the occupants knowing us or our parents was somewhat remote. Thinking nobody was home, we went into the yard to raid the tree. Albert and Tony climbed the tree and tossed mangoes to me on the ground where I promptly placed them inside a box. Unbeknownst to us, the owner had been watching us. He slipped out his front door and walked around the entire block in order to come up behind us. As he came up behind me, I turned around to see him pointing a large silver handgun with a pearl handle directly in my face at an arm's length. I panicked and threw the box up to my face for protection as if it would have stopped the bullet from blowing my brains out. The few mangoes that I had already collected, spilled out of the box onto the ground.

The neighbor told us he had been watching us, and had been waiting, because he knew sooner or later we would come to his yard. He then played the oldest, but most effective, psychological trick an adult could play on a child. He said, "I know you lil bastards gonna come back in my yard when I leave, so I should just blow your brains out right now and don't have to worry about y'all no more." I don't think I had ever been that scared in my life. I was shaking like a leaf, as all three of us just stood there unable to say anything, even if we wanted to. Our greatest fear was we did not know that neighbor, nor did we trust him. And, we all really believed that we were going to die that day. His psychology worked!

After scaring the life out of us, the neighbor made me pick up the few mangoes that had spilled out. He then told Tony to climb back into his yard and place the box of mangoes next to his back door. After that, he finally put the gun away, but before he hopped across the fence back into his back yard, he warned us that if we even mistakenly touched his fence again while playing around, he would shoot our heads off. Based on what we had seen that afternoon, we clearly believed he would follow through with his promise, and as a result, his mangoes grew in peace from that day forward.

Since our mango efforts failed miserably, Albert, Tony, and I returned to the job of selling avocados to the Cuban factory workers. The income was in no way comparable to mango sales, but we survived. Thanks to the avocados, however, we stumbled upon another job. We happened upon an older white man getting out of his car and going inside one of the factories. He asked what we were looking for while giving us that suspicious look that older whites would often give us. We told him we were not looking for anything and were on our way home after selling "applecottas" (as we called them) to the Cubans who worked in the factories. He then told us that he needed some summer cleaning help, and to come back on Friday to start working. When we returned to the factory that Friday, we walked in and found the man sitting in a small office and told him we were there to start working. He seemed surprised as if he never expected us to return. Little did he know how excited we were to have real jobs. I had been dreaming of that job since he mentioned it a couple of days earlier.

The old white guy told us we would be floor sweepers. We did not discuss pay but felt we would be paid decently. Between the three of us, we each had to sweep four to five aisles with large push brooms, place all the debris and dirt into large containers, and then take the containers outside and dump them into the large dumpsters.

While working, we noticed most of the products at the factory were little snack cakes and pies, and we would sneak and eat a treat here and there while sweeping. After about two hours of hard work, we finished the factory, and the old white guy paid us two dollars each and told us to come back again the following Friday. We were traumatized that all our hard work was worth a total of six dollars, so we constructed a plan to earn a greater return for our labor. When we returned to work the following Friday, we were given the same work assignment. This time, however, we each placed an unopened box of snack cakes inside the trash container, and dumped trash over each box, and when we needed to empty the containers, we threw everything, including the boxes of snacks into the large dumpsters. Then, later that evening when the factories closed, we returned, retrieved our boxes of snacks, and took them back to 56th Street for a serious good time.

This escapade went on for three or four more times, until one day, we demanded more money from the old white guy. He refused and really got upset that we had the nerve to ask him for more money. We felt we had a little leverage, because we knew no one else would work for wages that low. I then told him if he could not pay more money, we could not work for him anymore. My demand upset him so much that he fired us on the spot and ordered us out of the factory. Fortunately, we had already made a trash drop, and like clockwork, we returned later that evening and retrieved our boxes of snacks.

Since we were out of a job and there was still summertime left, Albert, Tony, and I did whatever we could to earn money. The hustling buggies jobs had started getting old because it had become so popular with all of the guys in our neighborhood. We discovered another mixed white and Cuban neighborhood, known as Hialeah, which was about a mile further west from the factory district. We also discovered that no one hustled buggies at the Food Bazaar in Hialeah. So, on Saturdays, we would walk barefooted, out of our neighborhood, pass the factory district, and about a mile further just to go to the Food Bazaar to work. The manager, Mr. Whitman, a large white man, was not a fan of guys hustling his customers, and he would frequently run us away, but whenever, he was not there, the other managers would always let us earn honest money.

One Saturday, Mr. Whitman attempted to run us away from the store, and we decided to challenge him. I told him we had a right to earn our money, and that the customers needed our help. He was not impressed, and chased us not only away from the store, but out of the entire shopping center altogether.

During our walk back to 56th Street, we were quite dejected that Mr. Whitman stopped us from earning money. For whatever reason, we decided to take our frustrations out by engaging in a favorite pastime. We would throw rocks at cars and when the drivers stopped, we would run away, but just in case they chased us, we would have devised a preplanned getaway route because we knew the area so well. On this one occasion, we had planned to run across a large cleared field about the size of a football field, then head toward the snacks factory and hide behind the trucks until it was safe to continue our journey back to the safe confines of 56th Street.

As cars whizzed by, we picked out a nice light blue car driven by a middle-aged black man and threw several rocks. The car came to a screeching halt as the man got out of the car and started chasing us. As we raced through the open field, barefooted, we were met by a huge surprise. The entire field was full of the largest sand spurs we had ever seen. First Tony went down because the sand spurs were too painful to his bare feet. Instead of stopping and dealing with Tony, the man kept chasing Albert and me. Then Albert went down, but the angry man ran past him, and kept his pursuit on me. The constant pounding of the sand spurs against the soles of my bare feet shot excruciating pain through my feet, but I was too scared to stop running. The favorite pastime that we thought of as a game had turned serious. Lives were at stake, and for the time being, I felt my life was the one at stake. So, there was no way I was going to stop running despite what my painful feet told me.

Finally, I made it through the field to the familiar factory district. I knew there was no way the man would find me once I got there. I went to the snacks factory and slid behind one of the trucks that was backed up to the building. I figured if he saw me and came for me, he would have to approach me from one side while I could slip out the other side and continue my pursuit to 56th Street. From my vantage point, I could see the angry man as he rounded the corner to where the trucks were parked, but he had no idea where I was. He then threw up his hands and ran back toward his car. At that point, I ran safely home. When Albert and Tony returned to 56th Street, I asked what happened to them. They told me the angry man ran past them to get back to his car and sped off as if he were still looking for me. That day was the very last day we ever went to the factory district or threw rocks at cars.

Chapter 16

Gator

Aunt Faye always ran with what could be called a motley crew of characters. They were always pretty free-spirited and loved drinking. One buddy of that crew was a guy everyone knew as Gator. He was tall and slender, and apparently had a heavy history of drinking. His eyes were always bloodshot, and his speech was always slurred. No matter the day of the week, or the time of day, Gator always appeared intoxicated, regardless of whether he was in that state or not. I don't think any of us ever knew his real name. He was just known as Gator by everyone he knew. As much as I tried to figure it out, I could never understand why he was given the nickname Gator. I always thought he and Aunt Faye had a thing going on but were not telling anyone.

I do not recall Gator ever having a job. He just seemed to go with whatever flow was directing him. I was also not sure where he lived, as he never talked about it. All I knew was that he and Aunt Faye hung together often, and usually, when Aunt Faye came to visit us, Gator would be with her.

One day during the school week, I didn't feel too great, and decided I did not want to deal with issues of school, so I told Mom I was not feeling well and preferred to stay home. I had to have been feeling pretty bad because I knew from previous days off that if I stayed home, the day would be filled with doing all sorts of chores, regardless of whether I was sick or not. For that reason, I usually got up and made the two-mile hike to school regardless of how I was feeling.

On this particular "sick day" from school, Mom was soaking clothes in the bathtub, and planned to wash and scrub them after they had soaked. She assigned that chore to me. We did not have a washer and dryer in the house, which meant we pushed clothes in a shopping cart to the laundry mat, or we washed them by hand and hung them on the clothesline to dry. On that day, we planned to wash the clothes by hand and hang them to dry.

Aunt Faye and Gator stopped by the house around noon, just as I was starting to scrub the clothes. After they talked with Mom for a while, Mom and Aunt Faye decided to go down to Buddy's Corner Store to get a six-pack of beer. Normally they would have sent me because during those days, I could walk into a store at twelve or thirteen years old and buy beer as if I were an adult. They did not send me, however, because Buddy and I had a dispute a week earlier. Buddy operated a bar-b-cue pit outside his store, where customers could buy bar-b-cue sandwiches or rib and chicken dinners. On one occasion, several of us children were playing around the pit, and somebody must have spit onto the ground. Buddy accused me of spitting near the bar-b-cue, and despite my sincerest pleas that I had not done anything wrong, Buddy told me to leave and to not come back to his store.

In our community, if someone forced you from his home or business, and said to not return, that really meant not to come back for the next week or so. The usual protocol was to wait until cooler heads prevailed, and everything would be okay. I was wired differently. If someone said don't come back to me, that meant do not ever show your face again. I took it quite literally. So, when Buddy unfairly barred me from his store, I told myself I would never give him the opportunity of doing that disservice to me again, and under no circumstances would I ever visit the store again. So, when Mom and Aunt Faye needed someone to go get them a six-pack, there was no option of me going to get it, because of the dispute with Buddy, plus they knew I was not feeling well.

Mom and Aunt Faye decided to go to Buddy's to get the six-pack of beer that they would drink with Gator. We lived on 56th Street, and Buddy's was on 54th Street, so the two-block walk there and back should not have taken more than twenty minutes at most. When Mom and Aunt Faye left, I was in the bathroom kneeling over the tub scrubbing clothes as instructed by Mom. Within minutes, Gator came into the bathroom, and playfully grabbed me while saying, "Get outta the way, lil chump; I gotta take a leak!" I thought nothing of it when he playfully threw me out of the bathroom into the hallway.

When he finished, he headed back into the living room

where I had gone to wait for him to finish using the only bathroom in the house. He then groped himself, and smilingly said, "Hey lil chump, next time I go to the bathroom, you better get out the way of this monster." I just casually said something like, "Oh, okay," and kept moving, because I was intent on getting my chores done before Mom and Aunt Faye returned, and I did not want to get scolded for not completing my tasks. Plus, I was anxious to get some rest.

As I headed back to the bathroom, Gator grabbed me in a playful wrestling hold from behind and said, "You think I'm playing don't you?" I knew he was playing around, because he always played around with us kids. In fact, I thought he played around a little too much. I tried to squirm loose, and said, "C'mon Gator, I don't have time to play. I gotta get these clothes done before Mom gets back!" He persisted in playing around and holding me in a wrestling hold, while saying, "I wanna see you get outta this hold, lil chump." At that point he pressed his pelvic area into my backside, as if to strengthen his hold, and at that very instant, I perceived a space violation. Then, he reached around and groped my private area, while laughingly saying "Yeah, lil chump, what you gonna do now? You'll never get out of this hold. I got you where it hurts." All of a sudden, I did not take Gator's actions as him just playing around. I sensed a very specific danger and tried my hardest to squirm out of the hold, all to no avail.

As Gator's pelvic area with an obvious erection grinded on my backside, with my private area firmly groped in his hand, he had given every indication that he was about to rape me, and for the very first time in my life, I felt genuinely afraid of him. Mom and Aunt Faye had been gone for about ten minutes, and I knew they would be back soon. What I did not know, however, was what Gator was going to do with me as he held me in a playful choke hold. I tried pleading with him that I had to get my chores done before Mom and Aunt Faye returned, but that did not stop him. I could not tell if he was playing or if he was serious. What I did know was that I was as scared as I had ever been, and I needed to do something quickly before things went too far. So, I told him someone was at the door, and even went as far as screaming, "Come on in!" At that point Gator released his hold on me, because he thought someone had in fact, come inside the house.

At that very instant, I bolted toward the back door as if someone had set fire to me. Once outside, I ran toward Buddy's Corner Store, but met Mom and Aunt Faye on their return as I was about halfway there. Before I could say anything, Mom said, "Boy where you running to?" At the same time, Aunt Faye said, "Did Gator need some cigarettes?" Initially, I could not talk, because I had been running so fast, and was in quite a panic. Then, I frantically spoke between breaths and said, "Gator went crazy! He was trying to rape and kill me, but I got loose, and ran away! We need to call the police, cause if we go back there, he's gonna kill us!"

Faye angrily decried, "That old bastard! He just wait till I get my hands on him. I'm gonna slice him in twenty-one pieces!" Mom then chimed in and said, "Just wait till I get to that house! I'll die and go to hell before I let that bastard come in my house and mess with my children!" She then turned to Aunt Faye, and said, "Faye, keep that sorry bastard away from my house and my children!" Faye retorted, "I'll handle that butter faced bastard as soon as I get to him."

Gator must have known that Mom and Aunt Faye meant serious business, because by the time we got back to the house, he was nowhere to be found. Our house was less than one-thousand square feet in diameter, so it did not take long to search every room and closet, only to discover that Gator was not there. Apparently, as soon as I fled, he left going in the opposite direction. We never heard from Gator again. He knew he had done something wrong and had violated the trust of those who loved him.

The shame of Gator's actions took a serious toll on me. I felt guilty as if I had done something wrong. I kept asking myself what I had said or done to trigger such actions from him, but could not come up with anything on my behalf that would have been a contributing factor. He had been in our lives for a few years, and all of us kids were quite comfortable being around him. He always wrestled or tussled with us. As a result, we never took him seriously. Plus, he always appeared to be intoxicated, even when he probably was not. From that point forward, I became distrustful of grown men who visited our house, especially those who drank a lot. If Aunt Faye brought a friend over with her, I would closely watch him like a hawk, but would never say anything to him or otherwise appear friendly.

Gator was essentially an overgrown kid, and that was

how we kids saw him. After that traumatic event, I started reflecting back over time to realize that he probably had been preying on us kids all along. I thought about my younger brothers, and whether they could differentiate between playful tussling and someone violating them. Without giving them too much detail of what happened to me, I asked each of them whether Gator had ever touched them in the wrong way. They each stated he had not done so.

Despite the fact that Gator had not been inappropriate with my three younger brothers, and that I was able to get away from him before he got too far with me, I still thought something needed to be done. I pleaded with Mom to call the police, but like so many other instances where we sought police assistance that never materialized, Mom was reluctant to file a report for something that would not be taken seriously.

Both she and Aunt Faye had zero confidence in the ability of the police to handle matters in our community. Unfortunately, her beliefs were warranted as we never heard another thing about Dad's killer, or all the times Mom's purse was snatched.

Chapter 17

Liberty City

After a summer full of adventure, entrepreneurship, and danger, the fall quickly came and it was time to go back to school. For me, it would be the beginning of middle school. Albert and I had become best friends and I looked forward to going to the same school he attended, but the middle of our street, 56th Street, was the dividing line for school boundary lines. Those on the south side of the street, were bussed to Miami Springs Jr. High, a predominately white school in the mostly white and Cuban city of Miami Springs, but those on the north side of the street, like me, were assigned to all-black, and non-integrated Charles Drew Jr. High in the Liberty City section of Miami.

Liberty City was quite different than Brown Sub. Almost everyone lived in two or three-story concrete apartment buildings or government projects. In fact, some of Miami's most infamous apartments and projects such as Lincoln Fields, Sugar Hill, Scott Projects, and Liberty Square (alias Pork-n-Beans) were located in Liberty City.

I was devastated with the school board's decision to use our street as the dividing line. We had no free transportation to get to Drew Jr. High, which was two miles away, while the Springs Jr. High kids, some who lived literally 50 yards away on the other side of the street, received free school bus transportation to their school, which was about the same distance away. My biggest problem with the assignment though, was the high school that we would ultimately feed into. Albert's sister, Keisha went to Jackson High in Brown Sub, and Albert and I both looked forward to attending Jackson as well. Miami Springs students were assigned to Jackson High, while Charles Drew students were assigned to Northwestern High, in Liberty City.

After Keisha graduated from Jackson High, she went to Florida State University (FSU), and was the very first person I personally knew to have ever gone to college. She was both Albert's and my idol, and we were determined to follow in her footsteps to Jackson High and Florida State. While at FSU, she sent Albert an FSU t-shirt with the famed Seminole head emblem. That was Albert's most prized possession, and had I gotten one, I would have likewise cherished it. That t-shirt was enough for me to commit to FSU in seventh grade, and as far as I was concerned, nothing would stop me from going to Florida State. Albert was of the same mindset. What I could not figure out though, was how I could get in the Miami Springs and Jackson High school zone. As much as we had moved in the past, I was sure sooner or later we would move south of 56th Street, which would allow the change to take place. In the meantime, I made the two-mile hike to Liberty City each morning.

I knew Mom was looking to move us out of the small rat-infested house, and my hopes were very high that I would be transferring to Miami Springs Jr. in the very near future. Despite my strong wishes, the wind was knocked completely out of my sails when Mom finally told me we were moving to Liberty City right across the street from Drew Jr. High. My world went completely blank! Mom was moving us into the very place that I wanted to avoid! I hated Drew Jr. and hated the prospect of having to go to Northwestern High. My pouting did nothing to stop the process, because within two weeks we had moved to Liberty City into a one-bedroom apartment. The apartment complex was a jade-green, three-story monster of a building that sat on 17th Avenue and stretched an entire city block from Northwest 62nd Street to 62nd Terrace. The corner of 17th Avenue and 62nd Street was commonly referred to as the heart of Liberty City. The building was humongous. I hatefully referred to it as the big green monster. What an instance of irony; Mom brought me directly into the epicenter of the very place I dreaded. That was definitely my version of the three Hebrew boys being thrown into the fiery pit. I thought only God could save me!

Moving to Liberty City was bad enough, but the 700-square-foot, one-bedroom apartment was enough to make even the most hardened kid break. Fortunately, I held on. The living room served a dual purpose as both Mom's and Jake's bedroom as well as a sitting area, while we squeezed a full-sized and two twin beds into the bedroom. By then, Craig was no longer living with us, but his sister Angela had joined us. She slept in one twin bed; I slept in one, and my three younger brothers slept together in the larger bed. Apparently, we were on a waiting list for a two-bedroom unit that was supposed to be available within a few months. Although we had lived in apartment complexes in the past, we had never lived in such a large building with so many people.

Over time, the Liberty City culture grew on me as I became accustomed to our living situation, made a few friends, had many fights for survival, and accepted our current position in life. Plus, the short trip right across the street to Drew Jr. High made the entire situation of moving to Liberty City, easier to accept. While I accepted the status quo, I always looked toward the future, knowing something would eventually change. I always had a hustle, whether it was selling avocados, used soda bottles, or plastic lace key chains. There was always a way to make a few dollars.

Once the school year ended, Mr. Stewart, a lawn service owner, invited Mavis's son Donny and me to go with him and assist with his lawn service jobs. Neither Donny nor I had ever done much in the way of lawn service, but we quickly learned how to edge and cut a lawn. Thereafter, Donny would spend Friday nights with us at the big green monster and Mr. Stewart would come through every Saturday morning to get us to assist him. It was hard work in the South Florida sun, but Mr. Stewart would pay each of us $10 for our work. The money was most appreciated because it got us out of Liberty City and was much more than the guy at the snacks factory paid. The one thing Donny and I noticed was all of Mr. Stewart's customers were white, he cut their yards on a regular schedule, and their community, and houses were outright beautiful. I recall one lady offered us a drink of water, and as Donny and I stood at her back door to get the water, I looked inside her house and thought how beautiful it looked. The cool air coming from her air conditioner just completely overpowered us. I said to Donny, "I wish I had this house!" Up to that point, I had never lived in a house with a yard and never had air conditioning. We relied strictly on fans for any relief from the brutally hot South Florida summers. The work with Mr. Stewart reinforced my decision to go to college. I knew if I went, I could have houses and yards like Mr. Stewart's customers, and wouldn't have to ever cut my own lawn again.

Once, while riding home from a long day of doing lawns, I asked Mr. Stewart how long he had been cutting lawns. He said he had been doing so all his life but didn't think it was a good business for us, and that because we were smart and hardworking, we needed to become businessmen. That was the second time someone told me I had worth. I had always felt a sense of responsibility and a need to take care of others, but to hear someone tell me I had the potential to do something major was powerful to me even at the age of thirteen.

Over time, Donny and I stopped working with Mr. Stewart. I wasn't sure if he just stopped coming around, or if we stopped being available. We did, however, still need money, so we started going to the few houses in our neighborhood with yards and asked the neighbors if they needed us to cut their lawns for them. Since we didn't have our own lawn equipment, they had to have their own. On a few occasions, some well intending neighbors allowed us to use their lawnmower to cut other people's lawns. The money earned usually paid for dinner for the family that evening.

Donny and I would also hang out on Northwest 15th Avenue trying to see what we could get into. The 10-block stretch of Northwest 15th Avenue from 62nd street northward to 72nd street was known as a very dangerous section of Miami. Interestingly, on one side of the busy thoroughfare was the Pork-n-Beans housing project, and the other side consisted of small stores, soul food restaurants, bars, pool halls, churches, barber shops, drug stores, shoe repair shops, beauty salons, and the city's black-owned newspaper, The Miami Times. The residents in that area relied solely on those businesses for normal day-to-day living.

Friday nights on 15th Avenue offered sights to behold. People would just hang out along the strip patronizing all the businesses. The sounds of music blaring, the smells of various foods cooking, and the sounds of couples laughing, arguing, and cursing was enough to make young, wide-eyed, and adventurous boys like Donny and me just sit on a stoop and take it all in. We were innocent enough not to get into any trouble, but mischievous enough to engage in entertaining activities, even if those activities weren't the most upstanding. Our favorite pastime was flirting with the prostitutes. They didn't take us seriously, and certainly, due to age differences, we never took them seriously. But it was fun to tell them how nice they looked, and how age was nothing but a number.

I recall telling this very light skinned lady named Champagne, that I was eighteen and wanted to marry her and have lots of children, and that she would never have to work another day in her life. At that point, she just stared at me, and then instantaneously, she began crying as she told me how much she loved me and had been looking for someone like me all her life. Little did I know that Champagne could cry on demand, and as she went into a very deep cry, the serious look on my face must have really amused her, because she then blurted out the biggest laugh I had ever seen, as she screamed, "Ah huh, lil Negro! I scared the hell out of you, didn't I? You were talking all that smack, but you know your lil young butt can't handle a woman like me, so stop it with that little bubble gum rap you got." Truthfully, Champagne did scare me crazy. I was only about thirteen, and she was probably eighteen or so. I did not know how to have an older girlfriend, or even how to have a serious conversation with someone that old. I just liked flirting but did not realize someone would take me up on my offer. I learned my lesson.

No sooner than Champagne stopped talking to us, a car drove by slowly. She talked to the driver for a few seconds, got in, and they drove off. As Donny and I continued our quest to find some mischief to get into, we suddenly heard rapid-fire gun shots, which caused everyone to run for cover. After a minute or so, people started coming out of their hiding places and everybody went back to doing the things they were doing beforehand, as if nothing happened. We never saw the shooter or any victim.

That type of activity was common for Liberty City, and especially on 15th Avenue. It was always amazing how we responded to the aftermath of shootings. Unless there was a victim where people could stand around and stare, like they did with Dad's stabbing, we would always resume normal activity once the shooting ceased. We were, however, very quick to respond to the sound of gunfire. I don't recall if I was ever taught how to respond, or if it just came naturally. Nonetheless, it became second nature to drop to the ground and look for cover whenever I heard gunshots. It was a very nerve-racking, but painfully necessary exercise that really was a matter of life and death. A slow responding person, no matter how young, how smart, or how gifted, was always subject to being hit and killed by an unintended bullet. Those survival skills were so ingrained in my mind that whenever I would hear firecrackers during holiday celebrations, I would become filled with anxiety, and unconsciously drop to the ground before realizing what happened. Many of my friends typically experienced the same type of anxiety.

On one occasion, Donny and I heard a gunshot, but because it seemed too far away, we did not respond in our normal drop and run for cover routine. In fact, we kept walking without even looking around to see where the shot had come from. Within a matter of seconds, we heard a bullet whiz by our ears, at which point, we took off running for safety. An old Bahamian man, whom we referred to as a witch doctor, lived in a storefront business that had been converted into his living quarters, on Northwest 17th Avenue, Liberty City's main thoroughfare. Despite our poor living conditions, we kids always thought it was odd that someone would live inside a business space as opposed to a house. As such, we would often knock on his door and run off before he had a chance to answer. On this one occasion, as Donny and I passed the old Bahamian man's abode, we knocked, but because it did not look like he was there, we continued walking as opposed to running off. Little did we realize, the old man was inside, and came to the door with his pistol and shot a bullet at us. Had we not heard the bullet whiz by, we might have continued walking without realizing we were targets for an angry, fed-up man. His second shot might have been more accurate.

Despite being nearly shot, Donny and I were not too phased by the occurrence. We had done something really stupid, without ever considering that the consequences could have been fatal. After running a block or two, we stopped and went about our plans to wherever we were going. We never walked pass the converted business again, and warned everyone that the old man was armed, and would definitely shoot anyone who knocked on his door. He was able to do what police or others could not do. Through his vigilante efforts, he found a very effective way to deter mischievous kids from banging on his door.

Shootings were so common in Liberty City, that I doubt if anyone called the police. In fact, I doubt if anyone other than Donny and I even realized or cared that the old man shot a firearm at a couple of kids. The older, rougher kids might have come back later to retaliate against him, but while we were mischievous, we were not criminal-minded, and certainly were not violent, although some adults may have thought so, based on some of the silly things we did just for fun.

Chapter 18

Becoming Disabled

Although, I sustained many childhood injuries during those days in Liberty City such as dislocating a shoulder while playing football, falling from a mango tree, and nearly drowning while sneaking into the public pool at night, none were as bad or as permanent as the injury I sustained that left me with a slight, but permanent limp.

One day Donny and I, and a couple other buddies, were engaged in a crazy game of throwing glass bottles at each other. Why we decided to engage in such stupidity as a way of amusing ourselves will forever be lost upon me. We had only thrown about two bottles at each other when Donny threw a fifth-sized liquor bottle at me. When the bottle landed, strangely, it didn't break immediately. Instead, it tumbled toward me as I tried to get out of the way. Then, in the freakiest of accidents, the top portion broke right before it hit me on the side of my right leg, just below my knee. The impact of the broken bottle hitting my leg caused me to buckle and fall down to the ground, as blood gushed everywhere.

I knew I was cut badly, but I did not feel pain. I told Donny to quickly go and get somebody. Blood was literally gushing from my leg and I could see muscle tissue. I must have lost consciousness because when I woke up, I was at the hospital with a nurse tending to the wound and Mom standing there beside her. According to Mom, once I went down, Donny ran into the store near where we were playing and told them to call police. We were only about a block or two from the big green monster, so he went there and told Mom, who came running to where I was lying.

Mom couldn't afford to stay at the hospital with me, so she took a jitney back to Liberty City while giving me assurances that she would be back the next day. Jitneys were passenger vans that had specific routes between Liberty City, Brown Sub, Overtown, and Downtown. They ran more regularly than the city buses but cost a little more. Since most of the residents in Liberty City did not have cars, jitneys were an affordable and efficient alternative. Mom knew the jitney system very well and could effectively travel between points within the city without any problem.

During my second day at the hospital, I received some very interesting treatment that I was not sure Mom had been completely clued into. After extensive examination of the wound by a white male doctor, he left the room, but within ten minutes came back into the room and asked if I was okay. After I indicated I was okay, he left, but within about ten minutes, he came back in and again asked the same question, to which I gave the same answer. About ten minutes later, he came back a third time, and asked the same question. For the third time I told him I was okay. Then it dawned on me that he was waiting for me to go to sleep. I had an IV in my arm, but I was nowhere near drowsy, and did not go to sleep at all.

Seeing the ineffectiveness of the fluid that was supposed to make me drowsy, the doctor went to get some materials and came back to conduct some tests. He told me he would be giving me some shots into my shin bone. At thirteen, I was astute enough to know that such a procedure would be completely painful. Interestingly, it wasn't. Instead of the needle being pointed like normal needles, it had a flat tip. He stuck it into my shin bone on three separate occasions, and although I could feel a slight discomfort from the needle going into my bone, it was not painful.

By the time Mom arrived at the hospital that day, the doctor had concluded his tests. He told Mom that a nerve in the side of my leg had been cut and that there would be permanent problems with my right leg and foot, and that I would not be able to have upward movement of my foot. He then gave Mom a plastic brace for me to wear and said the brace would help me to raise my right foot when I walked such that my gait would seem normal.

The brace was a small plastic item that fit under my foot, came over my heel, and then extended about six inches up the back of my lower leg. It fastened around my leg with Velcro. After trying it on at the hospital and walking around a bit, I was discharged, and Mom and I took the jitney back to Liberty City.

When I returned to school, I was forced to explain the brace to my classmates. Although it was not very noticeable, it could be seen whenever I sat down or whenever we had to change into our gym clothes during physical education class. Having to explain the brace was not that big of a deal, and it did make me walk a lot better than if I did not have it. The problem the brace presented, however, was that the edges that fit under my foot would rub against the inside of my shoes, and eventually tear holes into the insides of the shoes.

Since all of my shoes were cloth sneakers, it took no time for the brace to tear into them. So, I had to make a decision to stop tearing up my shoes or learn to walk without the brace. I opted to discard the brace, and I tried as hard as I could to walk without dragging my right foot and leg. Over time, I got better with my walking, and I tried to live as normal as I could with the disability. Every now and then, however, someone would ask me why I was limping, and I would blame it on my knees or pain in my legs or something. I never talked about my disability again, although that spot in my leg is still very tender and if touched, I would jump as if I had been shocked.

Chapter 19

Jake and the Big Green Monster

Thankfully, Mom's social security checks were always right on time on the third day of each month. Jake's cash from his day labor roofing jobs would always get us through the rest of the month. The problem was that Jake had started drinking way more than he had done previously, and Mom's drinking had greatly increased as well. Usually on payday, both would get quite intoxicated and start arguing over any little thing. Invariably, the arguing would end with Jake hitting Mom, and one of us would run to the corner store to call the police, since neither we, nor most of our neighbors in the big green monster had the luxury of telephones. Typically, the police would come, quiet everything down, and leave. As much as I hoped, they never took Jake away.

My relationship with Jake was essentially nonexistent. I never looked at him as a step-father but recognized that financially, he helped get us through the month. He was a very quiet man during the week. He'd leave the apartment early to "catch a job," and Mom would usually have a huge pot of black-eyed peas with neck bones, rice, and corn bread waiting when he returned. Or sometimes, she'd have lima beans with neck bones, rice, and corn bread waiting. On special nights, she would have liver, with rice and gravy, and corn bread, and without fail, every Friday, she would have fried mullet fish and grits. During the week, Jake would come in, eat his meal, and then position himself on the couch to watch old western movies. He never said much to me, and I never said much to him. We merely coexisted in a familial relationship that depended on the care of a common denominator – Mom.

On payday, Jake became a man possessed. When he got home from work, he would shower, shave, and sing a couple of lines from this one particular Spanish song over and over again. Once dressed, he would go over to the bar a block from the apartment, and later that night, he would come home ready to fight. We kids stayed out of his way, but if Mom was with him, they would both come arguing with each other. If she was already home, she would have had her drinks too. Either way, we knew it would not be a restful night in the apartment. Eventually, he would hit mom a few times, and the police calling routine would start all over. Whenever any of Jake's kids were at the apartment during this scene, they would laugh and make comments about the upper cuts and hard left jabs Jake laid on Mom, while my brothers and I would just sit there in the back room and try to bear it all.

Even after fighting with Mom, Jake would remain in a

fighting mood until he fell asleep. One night he started an argument with his son James, who was living with us for a few days. Unbeknownst to him, James had a small .22 caliber handgun and as Jake went to strike him, he shot Jake in the leg. The police and ambulance were called. Afterwards, Jake was taken to the hospital, and James fled the city. I'm not sure if James was ever prosecuted for shooting his father, but it is more likely than not that he was not even charged with the crime.

On another night, Jake went through the house looking for something alcoholic to drink. Mom's drink of choice was Canadian Mist whiskey, and Jake knew she would usually keep a half pint bottle stashed somewhere around the house. Since Mom knew Jake would seek out her stash, she would hide it in places Jake wouldn't think to look.

During Jake's search mission, he looked through the garbage container in the kitchen, and ah, there it was underneath the garbage, a half-pint sized Canadian Mist bottle that was a little less than half-full with what Jake thought was Canadian Mist whiskey.

What Jack didn't know about was what I did earlier that night when I needed to badly use the only bathroom in the house. Because it was being used for a lengthy period of time, I retrieved the empty bottle from the garbage, took it to our bedroom, urinated in it, twisted the top back on, and placed it under the garbage so no one would mistakenly think it was alcohol.

When Jake took a healthy swallow of the liquid, he

discovered that it truly was not alcohol. Since we had all gone to bed, he burst into our room with the fury of an angry bull, and demanded to know who tried to poison him! As frightened as I was, I explained that I meant him no harm and that I only needed to pee because the bathroom was occupied, and that never in a million years would I have ever thought someone would go into the garbage to seek out a hidden bottle of liquor. Obviously, my fast talking and explaining resonated with him, because he laughed it off and went to bed.

Jake's drinking would usually cause him to fall off into a very deep sleep and he would remain that way until the next morning. He wouldn't even awaken to use the toilet, which caused him to urinate all over himself multiple times during the night. Mom would eventually go to bed as well, and while her sleep was not as long as Jake's, it was just as deep.

On many occasions during Mom's and Jake's deep sleeps, Jake would awaken the next morning with all of his money gone from his pockets. He, like most people in our community, did not use a bank account. Instead, after receiving his cash wages for his roofing job, he would carry the cash around in his pocket until it was all gone, which was usually until the middle of the next week. He quietly accused his daughter Angela, who had come to live with us, but for some reason, would never confront her.

Not confronting Angela was a fortunate decision, because we later discovered through rumors that a guy named Teddy who lived in the apartments knew how to quietly break into our apartment, rob Jake, and quickly exit. We had a window right next to front door, that had removable plates, and all one had to do to get inside the apartment was to remove one of the plates, and stick his hand inside to unlock the door. Since Mom and Jake slept in the front room, and we kids were in the back, we never knew anyone entered the apartment. Mom called the police a couple of times, but they acted disinterested, and nothing ever came of the police visits.

Once we figured Teddy was the culprit, my brother Tony and I concocted a plan to not only catch Teddy, but to make sure he never robbed us again. We figured we would boil a pot of Red Devil lye, hide behind the door and splash it in his face when he walked into the house. During that time, throwing lye or "pot ash" as we knew it, was a popular weapon in our poor community. It was supposed to be used to unclog drains, but many people knew if boiled in water, it would cause severe burn damage to anyone coming in contact with it.

Like clockwork, after Jake and Mom and the rest of the house had gone to bed, Tony and I heard someone removing one of the glass plates from the window. The unheated pot of lye was already on the stove, but when I slipped into the kitchen to turn on the gas stove, the embers lit up the otherwise dark room, and Teddy ran away. The next morning, Mom called the police, whereupon they finally sent out a fingerprint detective, who was able to determine that Teddy's prints were all over the glass plate that had not been replaced in the window. He was arrested for the attempted burglary, as well as violation of probation. We never had break-ins again.

After a year of living in the big green monster, we finally

got approved to move upstairs into a 2-bedroom apartment. Boy, were we happy! Other than having an additional bedroom, the apartment was basically the same as the one-bedroom unit, but since the living room did not have to double as a bedroom, the space sure felt much larger. By then, I had finished junior high, and reluctantly headed further into Liberty City to attend Northwestern High. My hope of attending Jackson High in Brown Sub was forever gone.

The daily walk to Northwestern was only about a mile, but that mile traversed through Miami's infamous "Pork-n-Beans" housing project. The official name of the sprawling project was Liberty Square, but most blacks in Miami referred to it by its nickname. I had heard so much about the Pork-n-Beans, and none of it was flattering. Many of my classmates from Drew Jr. High lived there, and regularly they would tell us stories about people getting shot, attacked, raped, and robbed. Although that appeared to be the norm for Liberty City, it just seemed so much more intense in the Pork-n-Beans. The big green monster was located a block from the Pork-n-Beans, so I was always right there in its shadow, but made a conscious effort not to hang out over there for fear, primarily of the unknown.

Like Drew Jr., Northwestern was another one of those schools that was not a part of the school board's busing and integration plan. While there were some students from the Pork-n-Beans who were bussed to Miami Springs High, no students from Miami Springs were bussed to Northwestern. Interestingly, we all recognized that the decision to not send white kids to the Liberty City schools was probably a good decision.

I got to Northwestern as a kid with no real direction in life. I knew I wanted to go to college, but I did not know what I needed to do to prepare myself for such. Most of my classes were very basic, and a couple were even remedial in nature. I had a lot of fights that first year, because that's what you needed to do to avoid being bullied.

On the weekends, I looked for ways to earn money. I longed for the days of cutting lawns with Mr. Stewart, but had no way of getting in touch with him. I was too old to hustle bottles, and the thought of hustling buggies at the supermarket had gotten old to me. The only option I had for earning money was cleaning Ms. Goodloe's apartment. She was a quiet older lady, who lived with her dog in one of the 2-bedroom apartments in the big green monster.

Everybody in the complex respected Ms. Goodloe and stopped whatever they were doing to say hello whenever she passed by. She never stopped to talk, but would kindly say hello and keep going. Every now and then, she would tell the guys shooting dice (or craps as we called it) that it was not nice for them to engage in such devil's play. They would just kindly say okay and pause their action until she passed, at which point they would proceed with the gambling. Never, however, did they disobey Ms. Goodloe or say something disrespectful to her. She had indeed earned emeritus status at the big green monster.

On several occasions, Ms. Goodloe would ask me to run

to the corner store for her to pick up small items, such as sugar, or flour. I would quickly run next door to Joe's Store, make the purchase and get back to her within a matter of minutes, whereupon she would comment about how quick I returned. She would then give me a $1.00 tip, which would always come in handy for candy, cookies or potato chips. One day, Ms. Goodloe passed our apartment and saw me doing chores. She stopped and talked to Mom and asked if I did good work, to which Mom proudly said I was very smart.

During those days, the word "smart" had many different meanings. If a person was sarcastic, that was considered a bad kind of smart; if the person was academically inclined, that was considered a good kind of smart, and if a person could do a very good job cleaning and taking care of the house, that too was considered a good kind of smart. She then told Mom she would pay me to clean her house every now and then. When Mom told me, I quickly accepted. The job consisted of sweeping, dusting, and wiping down cabinets and doors. It was pretty easy work for the five dollars payment.

Oftentimes during the cleanings, Ms. Goodloe would ask me what I wanted to do when I grew up. I always said I wanted to be a teacher because I liked to read, and I always visualized myself standing in front of a class and teaching young boys and girls. She thought that was a good idea but would always say she saw a lawyer in me. Although the TV program, the Perry Mason Show, was my favorite show, I never thought of myself actually being a lawyer. My struggles at the time were just too big and the poverty too great. Nevertheless Ms.

Goodloe persisted that I become a lawyer.

By the time I reached high school, the Jake crap had become too much to bear. The same old story kept repeating itself over and over again. He would get drunk, raise hell, and beat Mom. I had put up with this for years, even to the point that I tried to figure how I could get out of my family, or worse, my life. I even started writing small comments on the walls in places that my family would not look to find them. I would actually write the date, and say something such as, "6/1/74 – Somebody please rescue me. I can't take this anymore. I hate this place, I hate this life." This was probably akin to writing in a diary. It would calm me down for the moment.

Everything with Jake finally changed one particular Friday night. Jake, as usual, was arguing with Mom, and he went into the kitchen and grabbed a knife. Right then, my mind immediately flashed back to George grabbing a knife before killing Dad. As Jake stood in the kitchen, I jumped in front of him and said "Jake, please leave! I'm tired of this shit!' Before I knew what happened, Jake slapped me so hard that I fell back out of the kitchen and tumbled over an item of furniture in the living room. He then stood over me with the large knife pointed directly at me and said, "Boy, if you ever get in my face again, I will gut you like a fish!"

Maybe I did not take Jake's threat seriously, or maybe my situation was so depressing that I actually wanted him to in fact gut me like a fish. I was not sure which emotion took over, but instinctively, I stood up and shouted, "Well, anybody can talk bad when they have a butcher knife in their hand." At that precise moment, Jake threw the knife onto the floor, and before I realized what was happening, I charged him as if I was shot from a cannon, and swung, swung, and swung as if my life depended on it. Actually, my life did depend on it, because if he could, I'm sure Jake would have killed me that evening. Instead, he posed no defense at all. For a few seconds, I was a world champion fighter, and he was a helpless contender with no hope for survival. I literally bombarded him with hit after hit.

After Jake fell down, I made sure the knife was not near him, as I continued beating him. Granted, he was pretty intoxicated, and probably could not defend himself from anyone, but I did not care. I had eight years of frustration, fear, hunger, disappointment, resentment, and hatred built up inside of me, and it all came gushing out as I laid blow upon blow on him. For a fleeting second, I thought of taking the knife and doing to Craig's and Angela's dad, what had been done to my dad. I felt they needed to feel what it felt like to be without a father for the rest of their lives. At that very second Mom came from the back and shouted, "Stop it, that's enough!" As I pulled back, Jake got up and ran out of the apartment as quickly as he could. He took the stairs two at a time without stumbling, then got into his car and sped off to the sound of screeching tires and a louder than normal muffler.

We did not hear from Jake the rest of that Friday night, or that Saturday. I did, however, feel we would hear from him, and for that reason, I kept a good watch, and I kept the doors locked. As I suspected, two days later, Jake showed up with his son, Jake Jr. I was the only one at home at the time, and as I saw them get out the car and come upstairs, I froze by the back door, ready to run to safety in case they decided to force their way inside. They knocked two or three times, and when I did not answer the door, they politely left. As I watched them drive off, I thought they might come back again later, but fortunately, they never did. That was the last we saw of Jake.

Every so often, when I think of that situation, I cannot help but wonder what might have happened had they encountered me. Did Jake have another knife? A gun? Jake Jr. and I were not the best of friends. We were the same age, and were pretty cool with each other, and like his siblings, Craig and Angela, he had lived with us for a short time, and had witnessed some of the punches his dad landed on Mom's face over the years. Surely, he must have thought I would retaliate one day. I am sure he would have eventually retaliated had that been his mother. I always end my thoughts about that situation thinking how ironic it was that the person Jake would have ultimately killed, ended up saving him from being killed.

Chapter 20

Man of the House

After Jake left, we didn't have the small week to week income that was used to help get us through the month. Mom's social security checks typically took care of rent, clothing, electricity and the first week of food, and Jake's income would get us through the rest of the month. After he left, we had to stretch money a little further. Summers wouldn't be a problem, because I could work a full-time job, but working during the school year was a tad bit problematic. But, I had a family that needed to survive, so I had to do what I had to do.

Every now and then, I would take a day off from school to pick limes for pay. An old painted school bus would come through the neighborhood to pick up a load of people and take them to lime groves down in the southern part of the county. There, they would pick limes all day and get paid by the number of tall bushels they picked. Most of the people were older experienced pickers, who knew to bring gloves, snacks, lunch, and proper clothing to cover their arms. I, on the other hand, was completely green on my first trip. I had two dollars for lunch which I had to stretch as far as possible at the lunch truck. Worse, I did not bring gloves; nor did I wear long sleeves to protect my hands and arms from the prickly needles as I reached between leaves to pull limes off their branches. At the end of the day, I was battered, extensively scratched up, and starving, but I was paid about $18.00 for the bushels I picked.

I went back on other harvesting trips, however, it was usually during a school holiday and I was absolutely sure to be better prepared to protect myself.

The money was sufficient to buy enough food for a couple of days; unfortunately, the harvesting did not bring in enough money to keep the electricity running, which caused the power company to disconnect our service. At that point, we had to do what others in similar circumstances did. We had to borrow power. Basically, that meant, we ran an extension cord into the light fixture outside our front door and intercepted power. Since that light was used to illuminate the apartment's walkways, it was not connected to our power bill. We would therefore plug the extension cord into that outlet and run the cord into the house where we would plug the refrigerator, TV, and lamp cords into the other end. I would hook everything up as soon as it got dark and unhook everything before I left for school the next morning. The food in the freezer would stay cool enough until we hooked everything up again the next night.

The borrowing of power, as we commonly called it, was a common occurrence in the big green monster, as it was in many other apartment complexes in Liberty City. Sometimes, the power would be borrowed from next door neighbors, and the borrower would pay a portion of the neighbor's power bill. In many instances, the neighbors were family members, which made this practice even more prevalent. While the practice definitely was not legal, it was a means of survival for so many people who lived in poverty and worked as hard as possible to make it from day to day. We knew what we were doing was not right, but we justified it on the basis that our financial situation was too dire, and that we would have had to otherwise live in the dark and rely solely on daylight and candles. I do not regret our actions, and I am sure Mom did not regret them either. We simply did what we had to do to survive.

Despite our circumstances, I was starting to understand what was going on in school. I had no more remedial classes, and I was starting to like learning. Reading had become my escape from reality. Anything in sight would get read. Even the backs of detergent boxes, maps, or old discarded encyclopedias were prime targets for my eyes. Anything with words was subject to my inspection.

At the end of my first year of high school, I qualified for a full-time summer job, which helped the family tremendously. By the time I received my first paycheck, I did not realize Mom expected me to dedicate it all toward family expenses. I was after all, a teen, and craved to live a teen-like existence for once. I wanted to engage in some of the useless fads like my peers. At that time, many of the teens were getting gold caps placed over one of their upper front teeth. Some of the caps even came with certain types of designs such as initials, hearts, diamonds, spades, clubs, and so forth. All school year, I had been planning to get a gold cap with a spade, as in ace of spade, as soon as I earned enough money. The cost was $120, but the coolness was worth the cost. So, as I started working my summer job, I made the appointment with the dental office to get the work done. Mom, however, had other ideas. When I got home with my first cashed check, she asked how much I would be contributing toward the household. I told her I would be contributing large sums from my second check and the checks afterwards, but the first check would pay for my new gold tooth. In Mom's choicest words, she told me that I needed to help out, and there was no way she was letting me put "some gold mess" in my mouth. I held my own with her until she threw her ace card at me. She stated, "Look boy, I pay the cost to be the boss in this house, and there is no way I'm gonna let you put some gold mess in your mouth while we need food on this table. You either gonna help out or whoop me. Take your pick!" That was her ace card, because she knew I would not talk back or challenge her. Instead, I just stormed to my room, and figured I would lock the door until she cooled down and would then head out to catch the bus to get my shiny gold tooth with the ace of spade design.

    Mom must have read my mind because she demanded that I open the door, to which I refused. Then, out of nowhere, I heard something hitting the door. It kept hitting the door until I could see the middle of the door begin to crack from inside the room where I nervously stood. Then, I saw a broom handle come through the door. Mom literally beat a hole in the door and reached in to open it from my side. Once inside, she continued her demand that I contribute to the household. I persisted that I would not. Eventually, I slipped out the back door, and just ran, ran to nowhere in particular, but just needed to get away from the stress. Then it occurred to me, my two sisters were in Georgia living with Mom's mother, Grandma OnaBell. My oldest sister Janice, started out living with Dad's mother, Grandma Susie Lee, but sometime after his death, Janice moved in with Grandma OnaBell, and my younger sister, Renee, had been in Georgia since she returned after Grandma OnaBell came to Miami for Uncle John's funeral.

After running for a couple of blocks, I decided that I had had enough. I had been the only man of the house for about nine years. I had not had a chance to be a boy and really enjoy doing the things boys did. Sure, I had a few brief moments here and there, but nothing on a prolonged basis. I found myself sitting at a bus stop just profusely crying. I was not sure what brought on the crying, but it was heavy, and nonstop for a few minutes. I just needed to get something out of me, and it seemed that heavy crying was the only way to get it out. By the time the bus arrived, I had stopped crying and dried my eyes. I rode it into Brown Sub to the Greyhound Bus Station.

When I walked into the Greyhound station, the man at the counter must have done a good job of sizing me up. He was a rather large black man with a booming voice and appeared to be about Mom's age. As best I could tell, I had never seen him in my life, but somehow, he acted as if he knew me. When he asked how he could help me, I inquired about the cost of a one-way ticket to Quitman, Georgia. In those days, you could drop in on family at a moment's notice. I had not told anyone that I was leaving to go to Quitman, but I knew no one in Quitman would mind if I dropped in on them.

This big guy looked me over and asked why I was going to Quitman. Of course, I did not want him to know that at age fifteen, I was officially running away. I could tell the way he looked at me, however, that he knew something was not right. He then asked whether I had been to Quitman before, to which I said, "Only as a small child." Then, this angel from heaven said, "You sho you wanna go to Quitman, boy? Ain't nothing there for a young man like you; nothing but cotton and watermelon fields, and big ole rattle snakes. You will rush back as soon as possible." After hearing that, I tried to put on the best poker face I could muster as I told him, "Well, let me think about it, and I will be back tomorrow morning." Of course, I had quickly decided that despite the hell I was going through in Miami, I liked the city life much more than I would like the rural life of Quitman, Georgia. So, I caught the city bus back to Liberty City, and figured I would just have to bide my time until the right opportunity presented itself for me to get out of Miami. During that time, I did not have many friends in Liberty City, and I had zero adults to talk with. I just held everything inside and penciled my notes in very small print in discrete locations on the walls of the apartment.

By the time I returned home, Mom had calmed down. I

walked in past her without either of us saying anything to the other. After a few minutes, I went in and handed her thirty dollars. I then told her that since the next day was Saturday, I would go to the Woolco Department Store and pick out school clothes for us four boys, and put them on the store's lay-away plan with a sizeable down payment, and would make followup payments over the summer until the bill was paid in full. She thought that was fair and indicated her approval with a semi-smile while saying "Boy, get on outta here" with the wave of her hand. That was her way of saying "thanks" or "that's a good idea." While I still wanted that gold cap on my tooth, I settled for having done something substantive with my first paycheck. I spent the rest of my summer earnings paying for our lay-away plan and helping out with other necessities such as food or utilities. The desire for the gold cap for my tooth soon faded away as a distant memory.

    That first paycheck incident taught me some things about Mom that I had never really realized until much later in life. She loved me and my siblings unconditionally and went to great lengths to ensure our safety and well-being, even though she lacked the appropriate resources to do so, and had been physically abused by Jake. She put a ton of responsibility on me, but I can only surmise that it was out of necessity. Looking back, I can now see that she was building a man, and I did not even realize it, because I was wallowing in my own childish self-pity, and doing whatever I could to find the boy in me. My resentment for her holding the reigns too tight around my neck eventually gave way to appreciation, love and pride as I came to understand her trust and love for me, and the fact that she relied upon me to help keep our family intact when we could have fallen apart at the seams.

Chapter 21

Life in the City

That summer of my first job was really what I considered the turning point in my life. I had to show major responsibility, and had seriously started thinking about going away to college, to Florida State in particular. At the same time, I became preoccupied with thoughts of how the family would survive if I left. By then, my younger brothers were old enough to look out for themselves, and two of them actually went out with a guy before daylight each morning to assist him with throwing newspapers. They were a little different than me. Their level of responsibility was not where I thought it should be. They were easily influenced by their friends and were seemingly becoming a part of the environment we were being raised in, which is what I tried so hard not to do. Maybe, I was like them at that age, and just could not see it. Whatever the case, I was concerned. I started talking to them about making something of their lives, about avoiding trouble, and about doing well in school. The big brother mentor aspect had kicked in pretty heavily. Despite that, I had the feeling no one was listening to me although they were hearing me.

The remaining high school years flew by like crazy! I fell in love with the school I initially dreaded attending, made tons of friends, kept a part-time job, went on a few out of state school trips, became a member of the track team, joined school clubs, found a girlfriend, joined community organizations such as Junior Achievement, went to football and basketball games, went to the Junior and Senior proms, and in all other respects, became a normal teen.

Finally, life was good. The normalcy I had been seeking for years finally found its way to my doorstep. All of that activity kept me so occupied, that I did not have to think of mischief or other shenanigans that would derail my plans to go to college. Plus, the new friends I started hanging out with were smart kids, who talked about going to college on a regular basis. Strangely, they knew all of our teachers and counselors more intimately than the average student. In fact, they introduced me to a whole new world regarding academics, class rankings, and college applications. As a result, I became motivated to become a high performing student with plans to go away to college. I worked very hard to keep my eyes on the prize, although the world I lived in constantly provided me opportunities to do otherwise.

Despite the normalcy that I found in my later teen years, we were still dirt poor, and we still did not have the luxury of a telephone. Fortunately, Mom started receiving food stamps, which stretched our food a little longer into the month, and every now and then, Mom or I could find a way to bring extra income into the house. We were definitely surviving and doing what was necessary to keep our heads above water. Eventually, it dawned on me that somehow, someway, things always worked out, and we were never consumed.

As things would work themselves out in any given situation, I always chalked it up to luck and kept on moving. It never dawned on me that a higher power was at work or was watching over us. I was never wired to think that way. Every now and then, I would hear Mom in her room praying while lying in her bed, but other than that, there was never talk about a higher power. We never went to church, except for visits on Easter Sundays. Spirituality was just not a thing for us. In fact, other than Ms. Goodloe, I cannot remember anyone in the big green monster, or other locations we lived going to church on a regular basis. Many, however, would listen to radio evangelists on a regular basis, and send money to them in return for blessings they would supposedly send back. Or, sometimes a traveling evangelist would bring a tent revival to the neighborhood, and we'd all go just for the sake of it, but there never was a spiritual reason for going.

While all of us needed blessings, we all put our faith in other human beings or dogs to deliver those blessings, but never a higher spiritual being. Usually by 7:00 p.m. each evening, the most popular question asked in our neighborhood was "What's the number?" During the day, we would go to certain houses in our neighborhood to "play the numbers" in hopes that a number that was somehow connected with the dog races would drop. If the number dropped, the bettor won a significant return from a small investment. As I recall, a dollar bet would garner a $35 return. Mom had a set of numbers that she played almost every day, and every now and then, she would get lucky and "catch the number." Those winnings always assured a big dinner that evening or the next.

Other people in the neighborhood went to the jai alai game, which was legalized betting where men would play a game with a small ball that somehow produced numbers to determine winners. Others actually attended the dog races and legally bet their money in hopes of bringing home a payday. Mom never went to the jai alai or the dog races because she could not understand the betting system for either event. Instead, she focused her efforts on the numbers racket. She did, however, choose to deal with only those numbers writers whom she knew and trusted. She had had a couple of bad situations previously, where she caught the number, but the numbers writer did not make good on Mom's winnings.

The numbers racket was illegal, and everybody knew it; so was selling alcohol, but it was as normal and natural in our neighborhood as anything else. We sold and bought goods and services solely with each other, and everybody saw their business transaction as a way of investing in their tomorrows or their next weeks. Our idea of the future was making it through the end of next week, getting our delayed purchases from lay-away, or making our rent payments to prevent our white landlords from abruptly kicking us to the curb and padlocking our doors.

Interestingly, during those days, I did not associate going

to church with spirituality. I associated it with dressing up, looking good, and going somewhere to show everybody how good we looked. That's probably why we only went on Easter Sunday when we had on the best clothes our money could buy after a 90-day lay-away purchase. There was a large popular church right down the street from the big green monster, and on a few occasions, I wanted to go, but I did not feel I had the appropriate clothes to wear, and since I was not a regular church goer, I was not sure of any protocols that were required to be followed once there. If truth be told, I was downright intimidated. I'm not sure why, but I felt if I went to that church on any given Sunday, I would look like a fish out of water, and be exposed for my lack of regular attendance. So, to avoid having to deal with that intimidation, I just did not go, although from time to time, I really wanted to do so.

Chapter 22

Pro Football

By the time my junior year of high school started, the need to earn money was critical for me. I recall asking my history teacher Mr. Dickerson, a very soft-spoken older white man if he knew of any job prospects. He stated he and his sons sold soft drinks at the Orange Bowl Stadium during Miami Dolphins and University of Miami football games and queried whether I would be interested in doing the same. I quickly jumped at the opportunity. For every Miami Dolphins and University of Miami home game, I would catch a city bus to the stadium about three hours before game time, make plans to pay for a crate of twenty-four soft drinks, and by the time I sold the entire crate, I would have about six dollars profit. I could usually sell about six or seven crates through halftime, and after halftime, I would keep the last drink, buy me a couple of hot dogs, find an empty seat, and watch the rest of the game as if I were a ticket-buying customer.

Those Dolphins and Hurricanes games were the absolute best. I got a chance to engage in exciting work, make some good money, and watch college and professional football games that most kids in my situation never had the opportunity to do. During that time, O. J. Simpson played running back for the Buffalo Bills football team and was my idol. Since the Dolphins played the Buffalo Bills twice each year, I knew I would get to see the Bills come to Miami once every year. So, I knew no matter what, I would get the chance to see O. J. in person. I also saw Mercury Morris, Larry Csonka, Bob Griese, Franco Harris, and all the super stars of the 1970's on a regular basis. If the game was an early game, I would even wait outside the players' dressing room with other fans just to see the players close up and in person, and even get them to sign autographs. I would feel like a celebrity on Monday morning when I would show my friends at school a cap that Dolphins' wide receiver, Paul Warfield signed.

Strangely, I never told my friends about my Orange Bowl hustle. It was as if I found a gold mine that I did not want to share with anybody. Or maybe I thought they would not be too dedicated to the work. Whatever it was, I kept it to myself, and absolutely loved the time I spent alone. In fact, the being alone aspect was what I loved most. It was during those times when I started realizing how much I actually liked being alone. It gave me a chance to dream or to imagine myself in a world other than the world I was in, without having to share that information with anyone. After holding so much in for so long, I had become accustomed to not sharing much with others. I would just dream about situations, and if possible, try to bring them to life.

During those Orange Bowl years, O. J. Simpson was the planet's most popular athlete. On top of that, his Hertz T.V. commercial was probably one the most popular commercials on T.V. The sight of him running through the airport wearing a nice three-piece suit and carrying his overcoat and briefcase always gave me a visual of me doing the same thing. It appeared as if everybody respected him and made accommodations for him. For that reason, I would always wear a suit and carry my briefcase whenever I flew. In fact, to this day, I do not fly without wearing a suit, or at least a blazer, and I have taught my kids the same thing. Little did they know, I developed the habit from the O. J. Simpson commercial.

Chapter 23

Making Moves

Going to college was a big deal for me. When I researched the family background, I discovered that none of Mom's or Dad's siblings had gone to college. I could not find any family member, old or young, who had gone to college. My older sister, Janice, had not gone either. As I started making plans to graduate from high school, college seemed like such a natural next step for me, but I could not understand why I was the only one in the family feeling like it. I did not ask if anyone thought I should or should not go to college. It was such a simple thing with me that I just mentioned that I would be going away, and that was that. It was as if that was an automatic expectation for me, although I never engaged anyone in my family or my neighborhood in any sort of conversation regarding the issue.

Mom had some reservations about me leaving the city. She thought I should stay home, attend community college, work, and help take care of the family. A few other people in the big green monster asked me about the community college as well. At least three other students who lived in the complex were in my graduating class, and all three of them made plans to attend the community college. I was having no part of it. I had been salivating about going to Florida State since I was 11 years old, and I could not fathom not going as soon as I possibly could. I remember having a discussion about college with a few people from the green monster and someone asked me whether I was going to the local community college. Before I could construct a decent response, I frowned and shook my head in one of the most arrogant manners conceived while stating, "No, I'm going to Florida State!" I essentially responded as if I was insulted by the question. Immediately afterwards, however, I wished I could have taken the response back, because clearly, it sent a message that I thought I was too good for community college, although that was not what I meant. I was just so focused on going to FSU that wild horses could not have held me back.

My persistence in going to Florida State was not without angst. I thought about my brothers, and whether Mom would be able to keep an eye on them as I had done. What about my contribution to the family's expenses? I had essentially been the man of the house since Dad died and I believe Mom and I both privately pondered our concerns to ourselves. This would be a tough decision, but one that would have to be made, nonetheless.

When it was time to apply for college, I decided my younger brothers were old enough to take care of themselves, and that I could afford to leave and let them assume some of the responsibility I had been handling for the past ten years. Since I had not been sharing those responsibilities with them, I knew they would need a little time to catch up, but at 12, 13 and 14 years of age, respectively, I convinced myself that they had the same abilities I had.

I went to Mr. Greer, our guidance counselor, and asked for the application to USF. At that time, all of the state universities in Florida used the exact same application. All I had to do, was just check a box for the university I wanted to apply to. Mr. Greer gave me the application while uttering a comment about the University of Florida. I did not pay it too much attention, because the University of Florida was not on my mind. I was thinking only about FSU. While leaving his office, I saw a poster where Arkansas State University was promoting its campus. So, I pulled the perforated card from the holder, and on a whim, I applied to ASU thinking if I did not get accepted to Florida State, I could get further away from Miami as a consolation prize. Under no circumstances was I planning to stay in Miami.

On January 7, 1977, I pulled the trigger and dropped the applications in the mail, followed by a trip to Mr. Greer's office to ask him to send my transcript to both Florida State and Arkansas State. About two weeks later, I got a letter from the University of Florida indicating they had received my transcript but needed my application and test scores in order to complete the admissions process. I quickly made my way back to Mr. Greer's office to tell him that my materials must have gotten mixed with the UF batch, and that I needed everything to go to Florida State University as opposed to University of Florida. Mr. Greer gave me that look that Mom had given me before when she needed me to understand that Mom knew best. He then said, "Oh don't worry; FSU, UF, they're both the same. You don't need to go to FSU. UF will be best for you."

In a normal situation, Mr. Greer's assessment – that UF was better for me than FSU – would have been the best thing a guidance counselor could do for a student who would be the first one in his family to go to college. In fact, many students miss out on prime college opportunities because their guidance counselors fail to give them good solid advice on where they should consider going to college. My situation was very different though. I had been planning this opportunity for most of my youth. In fact, whenever the stresses of my situation got too tough, I would imagine myself at FSU, completely void of any of the challenges I was dealing with in Miami. I had never had those fond thoughts about UF, or any other school for that matter. For me, it was basically FSU or nothing… except, well Arkansas State, but even then, I had surmised that I would transfer to FSU as soon as I could.

I thanked Mr. Greer for his fatherly advice and told him that I had carefully studied the differences between FSU and UF, and one was a much bigger deal than the other to me. He still did not respond as if he clearly understood my plight, and since I felt he could somehow impact whether I got in at FSU or not, I let out a deep, but respected sigh, and said with watery eyes, "Look Mr. Greer, this is something I have been wanting to do all my life. My cousin went to FSU. If

I cannot go to FSU, I might not even go to college. Please send my transcript and scores to FSU." I lied in referring to Albert's sister as my cousin, but my desperation caused me to do whatever I could to convince Mr. Greer that FSU, not UF, was the university for me.

After my plea to Mr. Greer, he then told me that he had a good contact at the University of Florida, and based on that relationship, he felt he could get me in at UF, but because of my SAT scores, couldn't guarantee that same thing for FSU. He then placed his hand on my shoulder, and said "Son, I don't want to see you get hurt; I think you have a lot to offer the University of Florida." That was a watershed moment for me, because I really admired and trusted Mr. Greer, but I had been planning to go to FSU for many years, and as much as I tried to accept the good sense that Mr. Greer was telling me, I just could not separate myself from FSU. For too long, my hopes and dreams had been built on the prospect of going there. Finally, he gave me that approving smile that told me he was very proud of me, and said, "Okay, Cecil, but if you don't like it, promise me you will transfer to the University of Florida." I promised him I would, knowing very much that the chances of me wanting to leave FSU were about as rare as the snow we received in Miami, that January day.

Finally, in April, I received a letter from FSU indicating I had been accepted for the Fall 1977 quarter. When I pulled the envelope from the mailbox, I knew it was from FSU, but because it was so thin, I immediately thought it might be a rejection letter. Panic set in. I wondered, "What if it was in fact a rejection letter?" "What would I do?" Would I have to stay in Miami and go to community college? Would I truly go all the way to Arkansas just to go to college? By then, my palms were sweating, my hands were trembling, and I just felt flushed. Without saying anything to anyone, I walked upstairs to our apartment, entered our bedroom, and shut the same door that was still damaged from Mom's broom entry two years earlier, and did something I had done very little of in my life up to that point, and certainly something I had not done in quite some time. I prayed to God. It was a short and simple prayer. I just said, "Lord, please let this be my FSU acceptance letter." After that, I tore open the letter there in the privacy of the bedroom, and the first sentence said, "Congratulations, your application to Florida State University has been accepted..." I didn't see anything else. I didn't have to see anything else. I leaped sky high and screamed so loud that Mom thought I was being attacked. She ran into the room, screaming, "Boy what's going on?" I screamed, "I got accepted, I got accepted!" Mom had no earthly idea what that meant. She gave me a weird look as if she thought I had lost my mind.

After I wore myself out screaming about my acceptance, I decided to take my act outside. The big green monster encircled an asphalt parking lot that doubled as a courtyard, and when all the cars were gone, we played everything from football, to dodge ball to volleyball to four corners to hopscotch in that courtyard. Usually, any of us kids could be found doing something in the courtyard. I ran down to the courtyard to tell all the other teens that I had gotten accepted to Florida State, and like Mom, they seemed confused at my excitement, and did not display the level of excitement that type of news warranted.

Because September seemed so far off, I decided the kids at school would understand better than anyone else. Since we did not have a telephone, I held in my enthusiasm at home and waited to talk about my acceptance with others who understood.

Mom was not a big fan of this college thing. She never knew anyone who went to college, and she thought it was something that only white kids did. She could not understand why I would leave Miami and travel almost five-hundred miles away to Tallahassee just to go to college. The community college would have been fine with her. Because I knew she could not completely comprehend what getting accepted to Florida State meant, I excused her lack of excitement. I knew she supported me, but I also knew she was concerned about the future of living in the big green monster without me. We talked out a plan. My younger sister Renee had made plans to return to Miami with a six-months old baby boy, Dwayne, in tow. She could work and help out, or she could get welfare assistance, but in any event, she could help Mom. Plus, all three of my younger brothers had started working for the paper delivery guy. He would still come to the apartment around 5:00 a.m., and they would go with him to roll and deliver papers to customers before going to school. I felt everyone was being responsible, and it was safe for me to leave.

Finally, the school year ended, and I had achieved one

of the most celebrated milestones of my community – high school graduation. For most of us, that was the standard we needed to attain. It was generally felt that the other things such as work, military or college would eventually happen, and quite frankly, our parents were not as stressed in seeing that those things happened as they were with graduation from high school. Basically, the pressure was off after such a lofty accomplishment.

Although Mom was extraordinarily happy with me finishing high school, she did not go to my high school graduation. She never went to celebrations, and I did not expect her to go to that one. I was able to ride with a classmate whose parents would come separately. He wanted to have his car afterwards, so that we could have transportation to attend all of the graduation parties. Little did my friends know how relieved I was that many of us traveled to graduation separately from our parents. By doing that, I didn't have to face the embarrassing questions of my mother's whereabouts.

Chapter 24

Florida State

Finally, Saturday, September 17, 1977 arrived. That day will live on as one of the most memorable days of my life. That was the day I took an Air Florida flight from Miami to Tallahassee to begin my college career. I had worked all summer and saved money to buy new clothes, a gigantic faux leather (or pleather as we called it) suitcase, and a one-way airplane ticket to Tallahassee. Mom's friend offered to drive us to Tallahassee, but that would have taken way too long for me. I wanted to get there as soon as possible. Plus, I did not attend orientation, I had not been assigned a dorm room, and I had not filed an application for financial aid. In my mind, those were minor matters. What mattered most was that I was finally going to Florida State University. I figured once I got to campus, I had an entire week to resolve those issues before classes started.

The feeling I had as that plane ascended over the Florida Everglades was one of the greatest ever. I recall looking down over Miami and saying, "Goodbye Miami. I will never come back." I knew I would come back to visit, but that departure seemed too permanent at that moment. Other than getting my college acceptance, I could not recall ever having that kind of happy moment while in Miami, especially after Dad died.

Once the plane landed in Tallahassee's small regional airport, I retrieved my suitcase and set off for campus, not realizing that campus was about ten miles away. I caught a taxi and gave instructions to take me to the FSU Housing Office. When we got to campus and were directed to the housing office, I discovered that it was closed during that move-in Saturday, but an older student we encountered on campus told us that housing officials were assigned to the various dorms. He suggested we try DeGraff Hall, a dorm that housed FSU's Black Cultural Center and the largest number of black students. Sure enough, that was where we found housing office employees.

I walked up to the housing table and indicated I was there to check in. I guess I should not have been surprised that they did not have a room for me. Fortunately, the university had prepared for people like me. They placed three beds in an activity room at the end of the hall on the first floor for temporary housing and told me and my two temporary roommates they would be able to find us permanent housing before classes started in a week. I was patient. I knew I had not done anything to prepare for housing or financial aid. I just naively figured something would work out.

DeGraff Hall happened to sit near a popular white fraternity house, and later that first night, Murray, one of the other guys in temporary housing with me, told me he had been invited to a party at the fraternity house and asked if I wanted to go along. I said sure. Once we got there, the white frat guys started showing great interest in us, the two black guys. Murray was a transfer student, a couple years older than me, and possibly many years wiser. The frat guys initially started giving us beer and engaging us in all types of conversation. I was feeling great. There I was, a poor kid from Liberty City drinking beer and having good conversation with one of the popular fraternities at FSU. Before I could finish one beer, another member would come up and give me another one. This went on all night.

All along, I did not realize the frat guys had separated me from Murray. I was not thinking about Murray; I was busy drinking all the beer I could and all the frat guys were talking with me. I remember thinking, "Damn, I am one popular dude!" Finally, one of the frat guys pointed out a sorority girl to me and said, "Hey Cecil, that's Laura over there. Why don't you go and welcome her back to campus." I thought, "Sure, that sounds gentlemanly." What I didn't realize was the level of my intoxication and severity of my slurred speech. But, since I was popular all of a sudden, I went over to Laura as she stood within a circle of other white sorority girls, and said, "Hey Laura, welcome back to FSU. I hope your summer was nice." Maybe her name was not Laura, or maybe my intoxication level was too much; or maybe Laura just did not appreciate a drunk black freshman dude invading her space. Laura's reaction said it all. She just looked at me in a most disdainful manner and said, "Go Away!"

As I turned to leave, the frat guys who sent me over were howling with laughter. Even though I was intoxicated, I instantly knew I had been set up, so instead of walking back over to the group of my instant fame, I walked toward the front door to go back to the dorm, but just as I stepped out the door, the floodgates opened, and I vomited all over the front porch. It's safe to say I left my mark at the fraternity house.

The next morning Murray told me he was watching me while the frat guys got me drunk, and since he did not drink that much, he could tell they were humoring me. I admitted I realized what happened well after I embarrassed myself. I never visited that fraternity again.

On Monday, after my embarrassing first weekend at FSU, I headed to the financial aid and housing offices. The impact of not having a phone in our apartment back home during the period between acceptance and enrollment had really started taking its toll. I could have addressed those issues by calling the university, but whenever I used a pay phone to call, I would end up putting large sums of money in the phone to no avail. In those days, the operator would tell you a specific amount of quarters you needed to put in the phone for a specific number of minutes. The problem with FSU was so many people were calling at once that it was too difficult to get a quick call in, so most times I would just wait on hold, but the operator would still charge large sums of money, even for being placed on hold. So, I just gave up trying to call FSU during that summer.

When I got to the housing office that morning, I was met

with bad news that if I did not have financial aid, I could not be placed in the dormitories. I figured, not a problem; I would run over to financial aid and quickly resolve the issue. When I got to financial aid, I saw that the line was extended out the door, but I patiently waited knowing I would get a breakthrough. Plus, I knew that as long as I attended college, social security would send me a separate check made out directly to me. I had written the Social Security Administration over the summer, but since I did not have an address at FSU, I gave them the address to the financial aid office. Fortunately, when I got to speak with a financial aid counselor, she was able to identify that a social security check had indeed come in for me. She also confirmed that I had not applied for financial aid, and that the $125 per month check would not be sufficient to secure a room in a dormitory, or to pay tuition. She then told me I might need to go back home and come back in January once everything had been taken care of.

If ever I heard a sentence that impacted my life, it was then - when the lady in the financial aid office told me I needed to go back home. I had already promised myself that I would not go back to Miami. There was no way that was going to happen. I would have rather died first. The thought of going back to Miami caused me to start trembling with anxiety. I thought to myself that I had worked so hard to get away, and that there was no way I was going back. I then placed my head down in my hands as my eyes welled up with tears. Everything just went blank for me. All I could hear was this woman's statement that I needed to go back home. My trembling increased such that I could not even talk straight. I nervously mumbled over and over, "I'm not going back to Miami! I don't care what it takes, I'm not going back!" Somehow the lady in financial aid must have realized the serious impact of the decision she was trying to make, so she said, "Look, I'm gonna let you talk with Ms. Kweis. She may be able to assist you, because there is nothing I can do at this point."

I walked to the back of the financial aid office looking for Ms. Kweis' office. When I got there, I found a very attractive and petite lady who appeared to be Greek. When I got to her office, I assumed the lady up front had called and briefed her on my situation. She welcomed me in and very politely said "Have a seat." I immediately picked up on how nice she was, but figured she was trying to fashion a nice way to let me down. Then, in the most concerned voice, she asked me to explain my situation.

Although still somewhat nervous and flustered, I wasted no time explaining how no one ever instructed me that I needed to complete a financial aid application months before I got to school, and how difficult it was to maintain communication with FSU because we did not have a phone at home. The entire time I talked with Ms. Kweis, she looked directly at me, giving reassuring nods every now and then as if she had lived in my situation before. I noticed the more I talked, the more reassuring she became and the less distressed I became. In all eighteen years of my life, that was the very first time I had engaged a white adult about a serious matter, and because I expected to be summarily rejected just as the woman at the front office had done, I was still anxious. Ms. Kweis's demeanor and tone of voice, however, was quite the opposite of what I expected. She was very understanding and reassuring, and her non-verbal actions eventually brought about a calming reaction from me. Then, the homeroom bell rang! Ms. Kweis told me she would give me a short-term loan while she submitted my financial aid application, and that she would recommend me for a room in one of FSU's scholarship houses.

Ms. Kweis was an angel on earth! Within a short thirty-minute meeting, she graciously resolved all of my issues. I had a place to stay with money coming in, and most importantly, I was not going back to Miami. I was in hog heaven and I owed it 100% to Ms. Kweis. The very next day, I loaded up my big blue pleather suitcase and lugged it completely across campus to the scholarship house. Mission accomplished!

Gaining residence at a scholarship house was very competitive. The house I was referred to had eleven rooms. Ten of those rooms accommodated two guys, and the eleventh room was for the residence assistant. The twenty-one of us split all the bills, which was significantly less than the cost of a regular dormitory room, and the only requirement was that each resident had to assist with cooking or chores. I always volunteered to clean up after dinner, which was well worth the low rate I was paying. Fortunately, the scholarship house had a last-minute cancellation, which paved the way for me to gain entry. I remember thinking I could not have had any greater luck in securing that deal.

Later that week, during orientation, I finally understood that I had been accepted into a special admissions program that was designed to increase the number of black and Hispanic students at FSU. Many of us in the program were first-generation college students who grew up in one-parent households in urban environments. Many of us, including myself, may not have gotten accepted to FSU were it not for the program. Although my grades were pretty high, my one-time SAT score was horrible and I didn't take the test a second or third time because I was not sure the score would improve. What I did know, however, was that if given a chance to succeed at FSU, I would put forth a great effort to do so. I found many of the other students in the program to have had the same outlook. Many of us were driven, not so much because we were naturally highly motivated, but because we did not have other options had we failed. I often thought if I failed, where would I go? What would I do? Would other chances become available? The outlook was usually pretty bleak. So, instead of focusing on failing or falling down, I focused on doing the absolute best I could as if it was the last chance of survival I had.

My roommate that first quarter at FSU was a white guy who was also a freshman. During our conversations, he would frequently discuss his exceptionally high grades and test scores from high school. He also partied quite frequently with the fraternities during that first year, and I rarely saw him study. At the end of that first year, he did not return. I was not sure if his reasons for not returning were voluntary or involuntary, but I do know he did not return. I never heard from him again, and do not know what ever happened to him. I always felt he had options if FSU did not work out for him, and that other avenues would keep him on his feet. Unlike him, I had no options had I been forced to return to Miami. So, for me, failure was not an option.

That first year at FSU exposed me to many people from around the country, especially those in the special admissions program. There must have been at least One Hundred of us in that first year program from cities all over Florida, including Miami, Orlando, Jacksonville, and Tampa, as well as locations outside the state, such as Atlanta, Philadelphia, Washington, DC, and many other locations. We took a lot of the same courses together, studied together, hung out together, and really created a quasi-family environment even though our dormitories were spread out across the large campus. Many of us had gone to segregated or predominately black high schools. We had not seen the likes of an environment like FSU, so having a built-in relationship with each other was critical to our success. Otherwise, alienation and ostracism would have prevailed to no end. Our program allowed us to thrive, exceed our expectations, take on major leadership roles, graduate within four or five years, and go on to graduate and professional schools, or the job market.

Florida State created an excellent model with our program. In fact, the university was at least thirty years ahead of its time with a diversity and inclusion approach that many universities struggled to emulate. They created a minority emphasis program, hired a black director who created a recruiting pipeline by establishing sincere relationships with minority guidance counselors and school officials around the country. The university then brought in determined first-generation minority youths, made sure the university addressed their housing, financial aid, and social needs, and watched them succeed. For all I know, we were laboratory specimens and did not even know it, but probably exceeded expectations over students who were not in similar programs. Over thirty years later, a similar program still exists at FSU, and the overall success rates for the students in the programs continue to remain at a very high level.

Fortunately, my acceptance to FSU came complete with entry to a program with many other black kids. Otherwise, I am not sure if I would have met many people. I had always been a slightly shy kind of person until I got comfortable with my surroundings. I was the same way at FSU. As it turned out, however, eight other students from my high school were also in my freshman class. Two of them were good friends, so I hung out with them most of the time, which made it easier for me to meet other students.

Chapter 25

Pledging

When I arrived at Florida State, I did not know much about black fraternities. I only knew there was a lot of secrecy and I had heard rumors about hazing. One of my high school teachers had secured a $500 scholarship from a fraternity for me, but other than that, I did not know much about the organizations. Despite that, I was very interested in joining, as I felt it would have given me that sense of family I missed out on while growing up in Miami. The problem I had, however, was that I did not know how to approach the members. They did not have casual beer-drinking social parties like the white fraternity I visited when I first got to FSU.

Instead, their parties were held on campus at the student union, where beer could not be served, and instead of standing around socializing, the students all danced to every song. Those parties were not the kind of place to initiate conversations about membership into their fraternity. In fact, the culture of black fraternities was such that one did not just come out and ask about membership at all. Instead, the proper protocol was for those who were interested in membership to express their interest by attending the fraternities' events, whereupon their members would eventually take notice, and if they were interested, they would discreetly mention something about membership. If none of that happened, interested guys had to wait and attend an interest meeting, which was known as a "smoker."

Shortly after classes resumed from the Christmas break, Alpha Phi Alpha Fraternity posted a notice in the student union that they would be having a smoker and encouraged all interested men to attend. Since I did not know any other guys who were interested, I attended alone and wore casual clothing. As I walked into the student union, and toward the room where the event would be held, I noticed all the other guys going into the meeting were wearing suits. What an embarrassment! I missed the memo! I had to act quickly. So, instead of walking inside the room, I kept walking past it, circled back around to the stairs and left the building where the smoker was being held. I guess it was a well-known fact that the normal attire for a smoker was suit and tie, but I had not gotten immersed in black life at FSU by that time, and I surely had no idea. I had a lot to learn.

Once I returned to my room at the scholarship house, I knew I did not have time to change clothes, so I figured I would just skip the event altogether, and break from the norm and approach one of the members on campus about membership. I figured at that point, I had nothing to lose. Sure enough, that following Wednesday, all of the Alphas wore their fraternity t-shirts like they did every Wednesday, so I stopped a member named Dwight and explained that I appeared at the smoker but had to leave because I did not know I needed to wear a suit. Surprisingly, he was pretty nice about it and said, "Oh don't worry. That happens every now and then." He then asked if I knew a guy named Lee, to which I replied I did not. Dwight told me that Lee was another freshman and would be the contact for the Alpha Interest Club, and that I needed to make contact with him in order to join the interest club. He also told me that the smoker I missed was not for freshmen, and it would not have made sense for me to attend anyway.

Although I did not know Lee, my high school classmate Sharon did. She told me he had an English class next to our English class, on the same days, at the same time, and that she would point him out to me the next time she saw him. That Friday after class, Sharon pointed Lee out to me. Even though Lee was a freshman like me, and was not a member of the fraternity, he had a group of guys around him which told me he was pretty popular with the guys and the girls. He was tall and thin, and wore a ducktail hairstyle, which was a popular fad at the time. I was a tad bit apprehensive as I approached him and introduced myself, but surprisingly, he was very receptive and gave me information about the meetings of the interest club.

During my first meeting of the Alpha Interest Club, I was surprised to know that the majority of the fifteen or so guys who decided to join were also freshmen. Most only knew one or maybe two other members. I immediately felt like for once,

I was not such a new kid. Most of the guys were somewhat new and relatively quiet. Realizing this, gave me much more confidence, and I noticed I started speaking up more often and even taking on leadership roles. The purpose of the club was to raise funds to help us defray the expensive cost of joining the fraternity.

The rest of that winter quarter, I spent all of my free time with the members of the Alpha Interest Club doing all types of fund-raising and running tens of miles per week in anticipation of the physical requirements we knew would accompany the pledging process.

Shortly after we returned from Spring Break, the Alphas posted information about applications for their Spring 1978 pledge line. Most of the members of the Interest Club submitted applications for membership, and then we just waited and waited to hear back from the fraternity. We would see the members on campus, but none would say anything about the success (or lack thereof) of our applications. The one thing that really had us nervous was the manner in which they eventually would communicate with us. Everybody except me lived in a dormitory, and each had a phone in their room. We did not have individual phones in our rooms at the scholarship house. We had two common house phones that were shared between the twenty of us, so quite naturally, I was very worried that the call would come and I would not get it.

Finally, after about two weeks, Dwight, the member who directed me to the Interest Club, called me at the scholarship house to advise me that I had been accepted onto the pledge line and that our pledging process would be starting in a week.

Twelve of us were selected to begin the pledging process. A few who were with us in the interest club did not get accepted to begin the pledging process, and we never knew the reasons they did not make it. Nonetheless, the twelve of us who were selected were ecstatic on one hand, but nervous on the other, because we had no idea what to expect. One of the first and most important things we did was get our line numbers established. Each of us were assigned a number based on our height. The shortest guy on the line was assigned the number one, and I, as the second shortest guy, was assigned the number two. Line numbers are very important, and pledgees tend to instantly connect and even develop a personality based on the assigned number. I was happy and quite proud of my number, and nothing was going to separate me from it.

After the first week of pledging, the number one pledgee chose to discontinue the process. At that point, the big brothers, as they are known, told us to reassign our numbers, and that I would become the number one man, that the number three man would become the number two man, and so forth. When they gave us this news, I was dumbfounded and decided to myself that the number reassignment was not going to happen, especially since we had already bought shirts and had our original numbers placed on them. Plus, I had already mentally connected with the number two, and liked being referred to as "the deuce." I had no interest in being referred to as "the ace." So, when we met as a group outside of the presence of the big brothers, I put my foot down and told my line brothers, as we were called, that although I had become the first man in line after our first man dropped, that I would not change my number, which meant no one else could change their number. Instead, I was prepared to deal with whatever circumstances came my way, even facing the prospect of being eliminated from the pledge process. As fate would have it, the big brothers were testing us, and when they saw how we stuck to our guns and did not change our numbers, they respected our decision.

From that moment on, for the next several weeks, the eleven of us ate, slept, lived and breathed nothing but Alpha Phi Alpha. We had a daily schedule in addition to our full-time course loads, which included daily three-hour mandatory library time, and regular group sessions to learn about Alpha history, parliamentary procedure, poems, steps, and Alpha songs.

Finally, after seven weeks, the day came when the eleven of us were initiated into the fraternity. It was one of the best decisions I ever made in my life and those other ten guys who were initiated with me, or who "crossed" with me as we called it, became my brothers for life. Based on the bond we established, any of us would do anything for the other.

After I joined Alpha Phi Alpha, I instantaneously became exposed to most of the administrators and leaders on campus. Previously, I had only watched how the Alphas dealt with other students on campus, but I had never paid attention to how they worked with administrators. I was completely blown away with how administrators knew many of the brothers by first name, attended their events, and even solicited their input regarding student issues on campus. Whenever I was with any of the older members, known as a prophytes, I would marvel at how they were able to get access to university leadership. Had I not joined the fraternity, I may have never even gotten to know a university administrator or the vast number of students whom I had come to know.

Chapter 26

Finding Salvation

Pledging Alpha Phi Alpha exposed me to many things and changed my life in ways that I would have never thought imaginable. One of the biggest changes it brought was the exposure to spirituality. While growing up in Miami, I had never spent much time thinking about a higher being. I had gone to church with friends a few times on Easter Sunday, but because the church was always hot and crowded, and because it seemed like preachers just went on and on for hours, I had no real interest in church. Plus, going to church was not something we did as a family. In fact, the concept was totally foreign to us.

There were two to three churches on every corner in Liberty City, and we would pass them all day, every day, including Sundays, without ever giving any thought to visiting them. Conversely, I never saw the church members going out into the neighborhood recruiting souls and extolling the virtues of attending church. It was almost as if they took the position that we had to initiate the desire to come to church on our own. Whatever the case, the churches and non-churchgoing residents all peaceably existed within close confines of each other.

One requirement of the pledge process for Alpha was that we all had to attend church together as a pledge line every Sunday morning. It just so happened that one of our big brothers, Martin, was a musician at a Church of God in Christ, and since he had to be at his church every Sunday morning, that ended up being the church we would go to. At 10:30 a.m., we would appear all dressed up, and participate in the service until it ended, usually sometime close to two o'clock that afternoon. Three-hour services always seemed to be the norm for that particular church.

I enjoyed the upbeat services that the church held but because we were always so tired, we constantly fell asleep during service, especially while the pastor was giving the sermon. At least the upbeat music, consisting of drums, horns, and other instruments, along with great singing, kept us awake during the musical portions of the service, but as soon as the sermon started, like clockwork, we would all doze off. Of course, after service, Big Brother Martin would remind us that he saw us and was embarrassed by our inability to represent his fraternity with the highest level of dignity. He even quoted scripture about Jesus returning from praying and finding his disciples sleeping.

When we did not go to Big Brother Martin's church, we would go to the church where Big Brother Miles was the pastor. He is credited with starting the Alpha Phi Alpha chapter at

FSU and, at the time, was the chapter's advisor. Everybody in the fraternity knew him, as he had been a member for almost 50 years. He was literally considered one of the biggest names in the fraternity's history.

Big Brother Miles' church was not nearly as upbeat as Big Brother Martin's, but we knew no matter what, we could not under any circumstances fall asleep during service. We figured since Big Brother Miles was the chapter advisor, he could end our affiliation at any second. So, we wanted to make sure, we kept him happy at all times. As it turned out, Big Brother Miles was the nicest person we had ever met. After service, he told us to go down into the dining hall where a good meal had been planned for us. The beef steak with rice, and string beans, topped with sweet potato pie dessert, proved to be one of the best meals any of us had eaten in quite some time.

The one constant I started noticing as we attended church every Sunday, was everyone talked about Jesus Christ and how acceptance of him as our Savior brought about a guarantee into Heaven and eternal life, as opposed to damnation in hell. That theory really started resonating with me. The other concept that started resonating with me was that Jesus died to save mankind from its sin, and that he sits on the right hand of God in Heaven interceding on behalf of mankind, and that when we pray to God in Jesus' name, God will answer our prayers.

After I became a member of Alpha Phi Alpha, I did not stop going to church. I had gotten used to going, and to be quite honest, I was no longer intimidated with going. Plus, I discovered whenever I was not too tired from the night before, that church was a very enjoyable experience. As such, some of my fraternity brothers and I would go to Big Brother Martin's church every now and then, and sometimes, several of us would go to Big Brother Miles' church, which was considered the Alpha church in town, primarily because so many members of our fraternity worshiped there on a regular basis.

After I started hearing all of the God and Jesus talk, I reflected back on those years in Overtown, Brown Sub, and Liberty City when things had hit what seemed like all-time lows. I often thought about how we luckily avoided total destruction, but somehow, some way, we always narrowly got by. Back in those days, I wondered how the unluckiest family always found luck at the last second. All those times when Mom's monthly cash was stolen, when we were kicked out of our homes, when I was going from school to school, when I was being bullied, when alcohol drinking was rampant, and when murder and violence were prevalent, we always found a way to come through. We scraped by so often that I often believed no matter the circumstances, luck would pull us through at the last moment. I think that is why I always kept going when I could have easily given up. I always knew something would give.

My church involvement and exposure to Christian thought and the Holy Bible slowly started bringing about a change in the way I looked at my past life. I finally started thinking and then ultimately believing that all those times when we were near destruction, luck (whether bad or good) had absolutely nothing to do with it. Instead, I surmised it had to have been more. There had to have been some intervention from a higher power. My family did not praise or worship God, or any deity for that matter, nor did we go to church and study the Bible. In fact, we were doing just the opposite. Despite that, we were kept afloat on many instances when we should have been consumed. The more I started learning, the more I reasoned that it had to have been God watching over us. I arrived at that conclusion by a process of elimination. If it were not God, who? What? Why? How? Those were the questions I constantly asked myself, but could never arrive at an acceptable answer. I finally concluded it could not have been anyone but God.

The more I understood the attributes of God, the more I enjoyed going to church. The pastor's sermons started becoming the highlight of the service, as opposed to the music. I started taking many helpful pieces of information away from each service. For instance, once Big Brother Miles stated, "A man can always run out of luck, but he can never run out of God's grace." That line hit me like a ton of bricks! He was right, luck always ended, but as bad as our situation got when I was growing up, we always seemed to make it through. Maybe that was the grace that Big Brother Miles was referring to, when he stated, "Grace is God's unmerited favor that is given to each of us, even though we didn't earn it."

I was onto something. God loved me when I did not even know God! "What a reality," I thought. No wonder I was never consumed. No wonder people like Mr. Crews or the big black dude at Ralph's, or even the guy at the Greyhound bus station came into my life. Those were people God had already put in place to talk with me. The more I reflected, the more awed I became, and the brighter the picture became. I was a child of God and did not even know it. While I was rejecting God, He was carrying me and my family. He was granting both grace and mercy unto us. I dare say, He was loving me when I did not even love myself or my existence. Then, I ran across a poem that brought everything into clear focus for me. At the time, I was taking an oral interpretation of poetry course at FSU, which required me to research poetry. In doing so, I ran across a popular poem called, Footprints, which gave me the best understanding of God that I could have gotten at that time. The last line of the poem read as follows:

"The times when you have seen only one set of footprints, it was then that I carried you."

Footprints confirmed what the preachers had been preaching about, and what I had been thinking about. God had been with me throughout all that I had been going through in those younger years. I had not been doing anything to warrant any special treatment from Him, but He was there nonetheless with tons of grace, and even more loads of mercy. Thankfully, through my exposure to Alpha Phi Alpha, a seed was planted that brought me into the light of God. I became convinced that was a part of God's plan all along. Fortunately, I willingly went along.

The pastor at Big Brother Martin's church was Elder Smith, who was a short man with a big voice. Since I no longer fell asleep when I visited his church, I was able to pay closer attention as I continued to put the pieces of the puzzle together in my understanding of God. During one service Elder Smith spoke about providence and coincidence. He taught how nothing done by God was happenstance or by accident, but instead was deliberately and divinely orchestrated for our good, and for God's glory. That was an extremely deep sermon that had a profound effect on me. The scriptural reference was Romans, Chapter 8, Verse 28, which states that "All things work together for the good of those who love the Lord and are called according to His purpose."

Elder Smith's sermon provided another opportunity for reflection. As I understood it, everything that had gone on in my life was a part of an overall plan for my life, and all of the pieces of the puzzle would neatly fit together for my good, and God's glory. "What a revelation!" I thought.

From that point forward, I stopped telling people that I survived growing up in extreme poverty in Liberty City all on my own without mentors. God sent many people in my life to impact my actions. Some were there for a few minutes, while others were there for a much longer time. Plus, I had God all along, and did not realize it. At that point, I started acknowledging that God's grace brought me through a very rough period of my life, and if that were not the case, I would have been consumed many times over. Luck had absolutely nothing to do it!

Chapter 27

Navigating College

While I was having the time of my life in college, things at home in Miami were going okay. My older sister Janice followed Renee back to Miami and Mom got an approval to move to the Scott Projects into a two story, four-bedroom unit that could comfortably accommodate everyone. Renee had gotten married, had a second baby and moved to a different apartment with her husband and two boys, while Mom, Janice, and my three brothers lived together in Scott Projects. Periodically, I would send Mom money from my financial aid proceeds, just to help out. I even called the telephone company in Miami and had them to place a phone in the house and send the monthly bill to me. So, there I was a college student, and I could finally fill in the blank that asked for a permanent telephone number. It was quite a feeling of accomplishment.

Despite the fact that things had calmed down substantially at home, I stayed at FSU that first summer. I did not even go to Miami for the one-week break between the end of spring quarter and beginning of summer quarter. I noticed many other students had done the same thing. College and FSU had become my escape and I did not want to go back to the very place I had been desperately trying to get away from for so long. I knew if I was going to be successful at FSU, I had to keep my mind on FSU at all times. That summer, I took six credit hours. In fact, for the next two summers, I stayed on campus and took six credit hours to go along with the hours I took during the regular school year. I got so far ahead, that eventually I got on track to graduate early, but instead of pursuing that route, I made plans to start taking graduate-level courses in case I decided to go to graduate school.

The extra time spent at FSU also gave me a great opportunity to read and understand the university bulletin and course catalogs. I studied both books so thoroughly that I could usually tell other students what their majors and minors required, and which courses were available during particular quarters. I had essentially become a de-facto academic advisor, and many students relied on my advice. My model for success was to take twelve-hour loads each quarter, consisting of three challenging courses and one easy course. I knew which courses were considered easy courses, and which professors were considered easy. This was very valuable information. This type of scheduling allowed me and others the opportunity to participate in extracurricular activities, which strengthened the family feeling and desire to remain at FSU.

One very interesting phenomenon I encountered at FSU was the race dynamics between black students, faculty, and staff. For the most part, it appeared that black faculty and staff were happy to see the influx of black students on campus.

Many of them—especially the staff—had been working on the campus for many years before black students began attending FSU in the mid-1960s. They were an integral part of making us feel at home. The concept of taking a village to raise a child was so very much applicable. Some of them would bring us food; some would loan us money; and some would even provide a place to temporarily live if any of us were without housing. They all had great nuggets of advice and wisdom to impart to each of us, and based on their conversations as well as their non-verbals, it was very apparent that they were proud to see us at the campus. A few were a little stand-offish initially, because they probably viewed us as highfalutin because we were at the big white college. After they got to know us, they quickly saw that we were just a group of poor kids trying our best to get an education with the limited resources we had available.

Our relationships with black professors were somewhat different than with staff members. First, there were not nearly as many black faculty as there were black staff members, and most faculty members had not been at FSU as long as the staff. Black professors were genuinely interested in our well-being as well, but more so from an academic perspective. They wanted to make sure we were doing well in classes, and that we were doing the things necessary to graduate on schedule. Every now and again, I would get the impression that some of them went out of the way to show that they were not giving us too much attention over the white students. And then, there were always those black professors that every black student flocked to because we knew they were very open about race and civil rights, and would really tell it like it was without regard to the race of the students in their classes. Those were the ones we all kept in contact with over the years, well after we left FSU.

One professor in particular was a Muslim psychology professor. His class was one of the most introspective and thought-provoking courses in the FSU curriculum, and students of all races flocked to sign up for the course, although it was not an easy course. Black students felt a special kinship with him because unlike so many other professors, he very clearly gave a pro-black perspective in his lectures. A black female history professor was another one whom students loved. She was always reassuring and concerned that students had a clear understanding of American and Black History and made a special effort to maintain communication with students well after we had taken her class. And then, there was another black female communications professor who was serious about our success, and constantly preached commitment to excellence, while at the same time offering a motherly type of nurturing.

On the other hand, there were a couple of black professors who we black students sensed did not feel we belonged at FSU. That was to be expected with white professors, but quite unexpected from black professors. Those one or two black professors never did anything outrageous to give the impression they thought many of us were less than qualified to be there. Sometimes, it was just the look they gave, or the small statements they made in private. One of those professors once asked me, why I didn't stay home and attend community college. I immediately felt the professor was implying that I was not ready for a major university and should have gone to a community college first. I had heard comments from other blacks that he was harder on us than he was on the non-blacks. Some defended him in saying he just expected more from us. Others argued he did not think we were ready for a major college experience and was bent on proving it. Whatever the reason, I shunned him my entire existence at FSU, and never thought about taking a class from him or otherwise developing a relationship with him.

    The treatment from white professors at FSU was more deliberate and, in some instances, abusive. For instance, during one class, a white professor stood next to a black female, propped his leg up on a chair and peered down at her as she took her exam. I am not sure if he thought she was cheating or what, but his actions were undoubtedly intimidating. The student broke down in tears after she turned her exam in. She may have filed a complaint, because at the start of the next quarter, that professor was no longer at FSU. It was rumored that he was "on temporary leave."

    In another instance, a white male professor was alleged to have threatened and intimidated black male students for sex, and in another instance, after two black sorority girls came late to class dressed alike after participating in a sorority activity in the student union, the white professor said, "Oh we're glad members of the moral majority could join us today." They were the only two blacks in the class and were completely embarrassed as everybody else turned to look at them while snickering.

In addition to the sometimes negative treatment from professors, from time to time, we black students would get harassed by white guys. I can specifically recall one occasion where I was with two of my fraternity brothers and as we walked along Copeland Street directly in front of campus, a pick-up truck sped by and its white occupants threw oranges at us while shouting racial epithets. There were many other instances where shoving matches ensued due to not so innocent arm bumps as we passed. As best we could tell, most of the aggressiveness came from white fraternity guys. Maybe our intramural football and basketball rivalries spilled off the field or court, and into regular life, or maybe the bravado was heightened by group dynamics; whatever the case, we were always on alert that something could happen at a second's notice.

Despite the racial tensions we experienced, many of the older blacks at FSU often described much worse incidents from those earlier years. Fortunately, the university had a very active Black Student Union, Black Cultural Center, and Multicultural Center, that would bring attention to racial tensions. And fortunately, the university had a very popular black Vice President for Student Affairs, who assured that all services to all students would be delivered in a fair and consistent manner. The white staff members were committed to assuring that same fair and consistent service.

Chapter 28

Priscilla

During my third year at FSU, I encountered a situation that completely brought my world to a halt. One of my fraternity brothers was getting ready to graduate from FSU and we decided we would celebrate with him. The celebration started at his house where we all had a few drinks of Southern Comfort bourbon. We then left to attend a campus party and when we got there, we became the life of the party. We screamed fraternity chants, where one member would shout out a rhyme, and the other members would reply in unison. Because of my loud voice, I was always the main chant leader. Afterwards, the DJ would hype the party even more by playing music that was sure to get everybody on the dance floor.

In the midst of all of that activity, I looked across the room, and there she was. She was breathtaking. She was a petite, very fair-skinned girl with green eyes. She was stunning. Despite her very fair complexion, I knew right away that she was not white or Hispanic. I knew she was a black woman, and I needed to know who she was.

By then, I was extremely popular on campus. There were

only about 1,000 blacks on campus at that time, and I thought I knew them all, or at least could recognize their faces. But I had never seen that green-eyed princess before. Although she later claimed she never looked at me, I was sure our eyes locked for a moment. When I popped out of my trance, she was still standing there on the sideline, just watching everybody dance and have a good time. I knew I had to think fast, because there was no way I planned to let her get away. Then I looked to see who she was standing with. Aha, I thought! She was with Linda, a friend from one of my classes with whom I often sat near and talked. I then calmed down, because I knew if she knew Linda, I would have no problem getting her contact information. I also knew I was in no shape to coherently talk to her that night. Plus, the loud chanting, thumping music and crazy dancing was too much fun to pass up for what I knew would be serious conversation.

On Monday morning, I got to class early in hopes that Linda would do so as well. As soon as she arrived, she came over and sat next to me to talk about the fun she had at the party that past weekend. After a few minutes of discussion, I then said, "So, Linda, who was the lil redbone you were with at the party?" We commonly used the term "redbone" to refer to a very light-skinned female. To my delight, Linda stated, "Oh that's Lucy, she's my roommate. Well, her name is Priscilla, but we call her Lucy." I said, "Oh, well tell her I said hi." Saying "hi" was my classic but simplistic way of letting a girl know I was interested. Typically, I would send a card with a nice, but not too personal note saying something like, "Just wanted to say hi. I hope your day was fantastic!" That usually got their attention because all of the other guys had "raps," or "lines," or could really "mack." I had none of that. Just a simple line was all I had.

Since that class met on Mondays, Wednesdays, and Fridays, I had to wait until Wednesday before I would see Linda again. Sure enough on Wednesday, she arrived at class a little early, and came right over to me and said, "Priscilla said hi back to you." I'm sure the smile I flashed would have lit up the entire classroom if the lights were off. I replied, "Well I can send her another message, but I'd much rather call; can I have the number?" Based on how quickly Linda agreed and wrote down the phone number, I knew Priscilla must have told her to give me the number, but to first make me ask for it.

Later that night, I called Priscilla, and we had a great conversation, so much that she agreed I could call back the next night. Over the next week, we talked a few more times, but since we were not dating, she went on dates with a couple of other guys from Florida A&M University, which was right across town. Finally, I invited Priscilla out for a date. I thought it would be a stretch since she claimed she did not date fraternity guys or football players, but I figured I would ask anyway. The most she could do was say no. I wanted to take her as my guest to an inter-fraternity formal, where members of all of FSU's fraternities would be present.

My fraternity would usually purchase a ten-person table, and five of us would go with dates. I did not go the previous year, because I did not have a date, but I wanted to be there for that particular year, and I wanted the prettiest girl in the room to be there with me. So, I asked Priscilla to go with me, and to my delight, she said yes! Her answer was sufficient enough for me to start dreaming that there was a future in the making. So, I made plans to borrow my fraternity brother's car, and started planning for that auspicious occasion.

When I arrived at Priscilla's apartment, my friend Linda answered the door and invited me in. Within a couple of minutes, Priscilla came out of the back just dazzling and looking like a million dollars. The first night I saw her, she knocked me off my feet, but this night, I was just completely blown away. My initial thought was "Damn, how is this happening? I'm from Liberty City!" My second thought was "Ah man, I will marry her right now on this very spot!" Her hair was pulled back off her face which caused more of her beauty to be exposed. And those eyes, Oh my God! She flashed a big pretty smile and looked directly in my eyes and said, "Heeeey, I'm glad you showed up." I responded, "No, I'm glad you showed up!" We chuckled as we walked out the door to the car.

When Priscilla and I arrived at the banquet hall, we were directed to our assigned table. The other four couples had already arrived. As such, Lee, one of my fraternity brothers, commented that he was about to put an APB out on me. I apologized to the table for being a few minutes tardy, but playfully explained that I had to make sure everything was perfect for my princess. Since I was always the type to not announce my plans, I had not mentioned Priscilla to any of my fraternity brothers, and none knew her. She, likewise, did not know any of them or their dates. Since I didn't say anything, my fraternity brothers all looked at me with that - "Who is she, where is she from, and why is she with you?"- type of look. I didn't give up any information though. I figure I would let them simmer with curiosity throughout the evening. As soon as the event ended, we bid everybody goodnight as my brothers continued their quizzical looks about Priscilla whom they had never met before that night.

That first date with Priscilla was perfect! We did not kiss when I took her back home, but I definitely felt something could happen going forward. Over the next few months, she and I talked a lot on the phone, but I could not get a sense that a real relationship was brewing. She still had a couple of male friends at Florida A&M, and if they asked her to go out on a date, she would go. One of the guys actually lived in my apartment complex, and we would pass each other from time to time, but never said anything to each other. I knew I had an advantage though, because both he and the other friend attended Florida A&M, while I attended FSU with Priscilla.

Any time I would see Priscilla on campus, I would walk her to class or give other little subtle suggestions to students that she was my girl. During one of our walks to class, I casually asked how her two guy friends were doing. She slowed the paced, looked at me as serious as she had ever done, and in the softest and most sincere voice ever, stated, "I don't date anyone anymore." I almost dropped my books, but quickly pulled myself together and stated, "Oh, I'm sorry to hear that." We both let out a loud laugh, as she knew I was being extremely sarcastic. I knew Priscilla had cleared the way for me to become her man.

A week or so after our afternoon stroll, Priscilla told me she was about to go "on line" for a sorority and would not be able to talk with me on a regular basis. I understood completely, as I had already become a fraternity member, and I knew that process kept the pledgees very busy during the day and night. Once she started her process, she and I would chat every now and then, but I was patient. I knew no one else was talking with her. She was too tired. Finally, her pledging process ended, and she called to invite me to her probate show, where she and the other girls who pledged with her would be introduced to the campus as new members of the sorority.

Joining a fraternity or sorority was always a very discrete process, and as such, the campus typically would not know if someone was pledging one of the black Greek-letter organizations. Usually, we could speculate that someone was pledging if suddenly, we did not see them around as frequently. They were not allowed to tell anyone they were pledging, and in fact, usually would not socialize with anyone except members of whatever organization they were pledging. The process would usually last anywhere from four to eight weeks and would end with a public presentation of the new members. The public presentation was known as the probate show.

Among black students, fraternity and sorority probate shows were the most exciting events on campus and had been so for many years. None of the black students dared to miss a probate show, especially when the shows were put on by the most popular fraternities and sororities on campus. This process was such an important part of the social landscape that students planned their courses to avoid time conflicts. The stepping in unison, the singing, the rattling off of historical facts at rapid fire speed, the imitating of other black Greek letter organizations, and the official greetings to the big brothers and big sisters were all a significant and highly entertaining part of each probate show. No aspect of the probate show, however, drew more attention than the revealing of the new members line names. Those nicknames of sorts were given by the pledgees' big brothers or big sisters, and supposedly represented significant aspects of the new members' personalities while they were going through the pledging process. In some instances, the line names would stick, and literally become that member's name from that point forward, such that most people would actually forget the persons' real name.

While at Priscilla's probate show, the crowd gathered early to get good viewing spots. All of the other members of other black Greek-letter organizations clamored together in separate groups in anticipation of the introduction of the new members and the reveal of their line names. Priscilla was the number seven pledgee on her line. After the first six girls introduced themselves and their hometown, Priscilla finally stepped out to proudly proclaim that she was from Atlanta, Georgia, and that her line name was Red Pepper! Many in the crowd clapped. Some of her girlfriends shouted approval, but several of my fraternity brothers shouted my name in unison, so much that it took me by complete surprise. I tried to ignore them, but the big grin on my face was a dead giveaway, and many in the crowd, especially members of the sorority gave me quizzical looks. I denied everything, especially since Priscilla and I were not an item. When the show ended, I wanted to rush up to her to be the first to give a congratulatory hug, but my secret was out, and I knew everyone was watching, so I patiently waited until she had gotten all of her hugs, flowers and gifts from her friends, and members of other fraternities and sororities before casually walking over and saying, "Great show Red Pepper!" I think we were both kind of pleasantly embarrassed by my fraternity brothers' antics and went out of the way to play down any type of fireworks.

After Priscilla's probate show, the fire heated up between us, but neither one of us pulled the plug. It was obvious that she liked me, and even more obvious that I liked her, but for whatever reason, we were both moving very slow. Finally, on my 21st birthday in July, my fraternity brother, Lee, and Priscilla's sorority sister, Kristen planned a surprise birthday party for me, and they invited Priscilla. That night, she and I danced to practically every song the DJ played. Later I asked if she wanted to go for a walk, which she readily agreed. After slowly walking through campus for about thirty minutes, we finally sat on a bench in front of one of the dorms. I knew she liked me a lot, and I knew she knew I liked her, so as we chatted about things in our lives, I finally looked at her, and uttered one of the corniest lines ever. I said, "Hey it's getting closer to midnight and my birthday will be over, and I have not even had a birthday kiss. At that point we embraced and engaged in a truly passionate kiss. At that precise moment, I felt all of the challenges of my youth no longer seemed so great. For the first time in my life, it seemed God had sent me a person to talk with and to let my innermost feelings be known and shared. He had sent me a soulmate. I thought to myself, "Is this really happening to me?"

After Priscilla and I came up for air, I looked deep into her beautiful eyes and said, "I want to be your man." She replied, "I want to be your woman." After another less passionate kiss, I then told her, "Well that settles it, we're officially an item." She smiled back and said, "That's right Mr. Howard."

As soon as Priscilla and I decided that we were officially an item, I told her I had one rule that I needed to discuss. I told her I did not believe in the notion of "break up to make up," and that I was looking for a permanent girlfriend, who would be a future wife, and that if we broke up, there would be no getting back together. Maybe I have a built-in defense mechanism to shield my vulnerabilities, but I have always been able to permanently close a chapter without looking back. That is not a good thing, because everybody needs a second chance, but it is who I am, and I pray often for God to change that aspect of my being.

In an effort to avoid having to make up to break ups of any kind, I try very hard not to end relationships to begin with. To me, mending a broken relationship is akin to gluing together a piece of china that has been broken in two. The plate may be fixed, but the crack will always be there, and it will always be susceptible to easier breakage in the future.

Priscilla looked me straight in my eyes as if she was looking into my soul, and after a few seconds, she stated, "Well okay Mr. Howard, I will hold you to that." We kissed again to seal the deal, and on that night of my 21st birthday, I screamed loudly that I received the birthday gift of a lifetime!

It was only fitting that I got the birthday gift of a lifetime, because for so long, the age that I looked toward, and quite frankly, the age that I doubted I would ever see was twenty-one. But there I was, twenty-one and alive with the girl of my dreams. I knew God was at work

Chapter 29

Chief

By the time my senior year started at FSU, I was flying high. Graduation was in sight; I was president of my fraternity; I was dating the prettiest girl on campus; I was considering going to law school; and because I knew so many people on campus, several people were urging me to run for Homecoming Chief.

Typically, people compete for those titles with the support of a sponsoring organization, which in the great majority of instances, were fraternities or sororities. The rest of the student body did not tend to pay too much attention to the process. In fact, many non-Greeks loathed the homecoming election process and complained that it was based purely on popularity. As a result, they stayed away from the elections and left it up to the Greeks.

The Black Student Union sponsored me as a candidate for Homecoming Chief. Since most black students were automatically considered to be members in the BSU, that gave me a big boost with locating volunteers to help me and my fraternity brothers get the word out about voting. We knew we could get a great majority of the black student body out to vote, while the white candidates would rely strictly on members from the white fraternities and sororities. The results would be announced that upcoming Friday night at the annual homecoming concert that was known as the "PowWow." The university's homecoming week always had a Seminole Indian theme. The queens and princesses always wore feathered headdress, and the chief wore a feathered headdress as well.

So, there I was running for a position that a black man had never held, the coveted title of Homecoming Chief. The University crowned a black homecoming queen in the early 1970s and once they switched the title from queen to princess, they also crowned a black princess in those early years, but never had there been a black chief. After the dust settled, I found myself in the permanent history of Florida State University. I had been elected the first ever black Homecoming Chief in the history of the university. I was crowned during halftime of the Tulsa game. Life was good.

Chapter 30

Law School Acceptance

Within two weeks of the homecoming chief election, some of the news I had been waiting for weeks finally arrived. I received notice that my application for admission to Florida State University's College of Law had been accepted. I had only applied to two law schools and the first one was great news. I was going to law school! I could not believe that after all I had gone through, I was about to go to somebody's law school. I told everybody at home back in Miami, but nobody believed it. They thought no black man from the big green monster or the projects could ever become a lawyer. They had never seen such a thing. Neither had I. I didn't know life could be so good.

Two weeks after I received the FSU law school acceptance letter, the one from Thurgood Marshall School of Law at Texas Southern University arrived. That was the one I really wanted. Texas Southern was a predominately black university in Houston, Texas, and after doing some research, I discovered that the law school was a little over 50% black, but had a good number of white, Hispanic, and international students, and was considered one of the most diverse environments around. I had met a couple of Thurgood graduates at fraternity conventions, and after hearing so many great and wonderful things about the school, I really wanted to go to this famous place that was created as a result of the separate but equal doctrine when Herman Sweatt, a black man, was denied admission to the University of Texas law school solely due to his race.

As an undergraduate, Florida State had been fulfilling, and it was certainly a safe haven. I realized that for once in my life, I did not wake up to stress, anxiety, illnesses, and depression. Florida State and Tallahassee had actually done well for me. With all of my history of being the newly ostracized kid, I would have thought once I found a safe and secure environment, I would stay there forever. So, my thoughts on leaving might have seemed perplexing, but the more I reflected on that issue, the more I understood that all of the strife and pain of my younger years led to me developing a penchant for moving on before disappointment overtook me.

As I pondered my decision of where to go, great consideration was given to the fact that my relationship with Priscilla had gotten much stronger, and that I planned to make her my wife in the not too distant future. She was a year behind me at FSU. So, if I left and went to Texas, I wondered whether the demands of the first year of law school would be such that I could not see her as much as we would have liked. I wondered whether we would even have time for much telephone talk? I had read many books about law school, and loved watching the TV show, The Paper Chase, about a fictional first year law school class at Harvard University. So, I had a pretty good idea on how intense the first year of law school would be.

Finally, I struck a compromise on what to do about law school. I really wanted to go to Thurgood Marshall, but did not want to leave Priscilla behind, and I certainly did not want to put law school off for a year as my roommate Larry had suggested. The idea of spending a year in Tallahassee and making a few dollars did seem enticing, but I was impatient and ready to get on with the next phase of life. So, I decided I would go to FSU's law school for the first year, and after Priscilla graduated the following year, I would transfer to Thurgood Marshall for the second and third years, with Priscilla right there with me in Houston.

Chapter 31

Graduation

As the spring of 1981 wore onward, the date of my upcoming graduation from FSU drew nearer and nearer. As such, I found myself consistently reflecting on my journey. The past four years had easily been the best years of my life, bar none. For once in my life, I was finally able to let my guard down, I made and maintained friends, and I felt that people saw and respected me as a person, and not due to my circumstances. Over those four years, I gradually lost the notion that I was an invisible person.

Finally, June 12, 1981 arrived. The feeling was surreal. I was about to do something I had no knowledge that anyone else in the big green monster or the Pork-n-Beans had done. In fact, other than the friends I had made while at FSU, the only person who I personally knew to have graduated from college was Albert and his older sister, Keisha. She was the one who sent Albert the Florida State t-shirt when we were young boys. It was the shirt that changed my life, and influenced both of us that Florida State University was the place for us.

Pains For A Purpose

I had done well at FSU, especially being a kid who many thought was not even college material. Were it not for the special admissions program, I may not have even gotten accepted to FSU as a freshman. But FSU gave me a chance, and I, as well as hundreds of other kids like myself, took full advantage of those chances, and did not look back. I earned an overall B grade point average, and a B+ average in my major. I met my graduation requirements in less than four years, and even had an opportunity to take some graduate-level courses. And, I topped all of that off with acceptance to the only two law schools I applied.

As I was dressing that morning in preparation for graduation, I suddenly stopped and sat down at the small kitchen table in the apartment that Larry and I shared. I seriously needed to reflect. The years growing up in Miami had been pure hell and extremely painful. At times, it seemed like we were locked inside a revolving cage with no ability to get out. Somehow, we always escaped, only to make it through to the next crisis. Those crisis to crisis situations always made me think of other ways I could have gotten money or food. The temptation was always great to do the unthinkable, and resort to criminal activity, but thankfully, I always found a way to resist the temptation, or as I learned later, God always had a ram in the bush for us. As I mentioned previously, He carried me and loved me when I didn't even know Him.

When I came out of my reflections, I wondered who would be in attendance at the graduation ceremony to scream my name as I received my degree. I had previously gone to a fraternity brother's graduation, and it was so cool to see how his family members made such a fuss over his walking across the stage to receive his degree. As a matter of fact, all of the families were whooping and hollering to show their support for their graduating family members.

I sent invitations out to my family about graduation, but really did not expect anyone to come on my behalf. My family was not the type to celebrate milestones such as graduations and other special occasions. No one had been there for me for high school graduation, and there was a slight chance no one would be there for college graduation. I knew their not being there was not due to lack of support. It was more so lack of understanding that educational achievement should be celebrated. Because I knew that, I was not bothered too much. That was just the way we were.

My thoughts then shifted to my grandmother Susie Lee, who called during the week to inform me that she and one of my aunts would be driving down from South Georgia to attend graduation. Grandma Susie Lee, Aunt Punkin, and I were not sure how we would find each other in the large graduation crowd, so I concocted a plan for them to find my name on the list of graduates, and to follow the list as the names were called until the caller got to my name. They were instructed to watch me when I walked across the stage to receive my degree, and then follow me as I returned to my seat and to meet me at that location at the end of the program.

As I lined up with my class members to walk across the stage, I felt like I was walking on air. We were each given a small card to write our names and give to the announcer as we walked across the stage. The announcer would then announce our names as we got to center stage. I was nervous, giddy, happy, and emotional as I was about to hear my name called over a loudspeaker before so many people. Then, the unthinkable happened as I gave my card to the announcer and strutted across the stage with my chest stuck out as proud as a peacock. The announcer mispronounced my name! He gave it the British pronunciation and said "Sessell" as opposed to Cecil. I was so looking forward to hearing my name called, and never in my wildest nightmare, did I imagine I would get a wrong pronunciation on the biggest day of my life. For a quick second, I hesitated, as I wanted to back track and tell the announcer he mispronounced my name and that it was pronounced Cecil (See-cil) and not "Sessell," but I kept moving, still exhilarated by the stroll I had just taken, but somewhat dejected that my name was mispronounced.

The plan I gave to Grandma Susie Lee regarding how to find me in the crowd, worked to perfection. She and my Aunt Punkin found me, and I was ecstatic that at least two family members physically attended my college graduation to wish me well. After hugs and greetings, Grandma immediately said, "I thought this was supposed to be a college. They don't even know how to read your name." After a hearty laugh, I was immediately relieved to know that I was not the only one disappointed by the blunder.

After entertaining Grandma Susie Lee and Aunt Punkin for a short period of time, they left and drove back to Georgia. I then had the rest of the afternoon and evening to celebrate with Priscilla, my fraternity brothers, and other friends. Many other students who came into the special admissions program with me four years earlier also graduated. Our graduation was such a major milestone for us. Most of us were the first in our families to go to college, when many thought we could not get into college or succeed once we got there. We worked hard and got out within four years when the average for the remainder of the campus was five or more years.

I did not want that warm June graduation day in Tallahassee, Florida to end. The more I thought about my accomplishment, the more I reflected on how far I had come. Situation after situation regarding those early years kept coming to mind, but I kept saying to anyone who would listen that, "I made it through, I made it through," meaning, I made it through an extremely difficult time of my life without giving up when giving up would have been so easy to do.

In the midst of the euphoria of the day, I kept thinking about the times we got kicked out of our houses. I remember saying to myself that I now had a college degree and I would make sure we never got kicked out of our house ever again. At that point, I sincerely believed the degree was my shield and protector against the hurt, abuse, and humiliation I had suffered as a child.

The post-graduation celebration went well into the night. Cookouts, parties, dinners, gifts, congratulatory hugs, and fraternity step shows were all over the place. I expected the feeling of euphoria, but it never occurred to me that friends would truly honor me. I remember thinking what a difference a few years made when I was harassed because of our living situation. If ever there was a day when the world made me feel special, it was definitely graduation day.

Chapter 32

Reflections

Many kids growing up in the environment that I came from typically go through life with the same morbid outlook that I held. They could not see the forest for the trees. Instead, all they saw were roadblocks to what they perceived was a good way of life. Many did whatever they could to escape their circumstances, and many of those things ended up being illegal or immoral.

The truth of the matter is, many young men in situations similar to mine did not expect to make it to age twenty-one without being killed or imprisoned. They felt hopeless and that their life or liberty would be unfairly or illegally taken, despite their best efforts to stay afloat.

During those dark years, I often wondered if my family was cursed, or if someone or something had placed some type of spell on us. Nothing ever seemed to go our way. Even the small victories would sometimes seem short-lived. Or, as cliché as it sounds, one step forward would invariably be met with two steps backwards.

Pains For A Purpose

I remember how I wished for my father almost daily, and how I would see other dads with their kids and would imagine myself being in their families. Television shows such as My Three Sons, The Brady Bunch and The Andy Griffin Show ended up being my escape routes to fantasy-land, because they all featured fathers with their children.

Although many of us did not have fathers around, we had many surrogates who were our teachers, coaches, barbers, the guys who would give us small jobs, or the men who were always around dispensing wisdom and advice. Mr. Crews was the best father figure, but he was my teacher for only one year. After that one year, I transferred schools, and lost contact with him.

Unfortunately, those men I needed in my life were not consistently around on a daily basis. Instead, the men many of us young black boys regularly saw, and who yielded the most influence, were the ones we probably needed to be around the least. Those were the older guys who may have dropped out of school, may have dabbled in petty crimes, may have sold drugs, or may have had children they were not taking care of. Unfortunately, they were the ones we looked up to. They set the example, which in many instances were not good examples.

Despite the absence of a strong male role model in my early life, I never strayed too far off course, although from time to time, I did stray a tad bit. I always had a good sense for distinguishing right from wrong and would never let the wrongs I committed go too far left. It was as if I had some type of built-in barometer that would warn me whenever the needle moved too far toward an extreme. As I look back, I cannot help but imagine what would have happened to me had I not had that built-in warning system.

I truly believe God was ordering my steps during those times, and I really believe He in his capacity as the Holy Spirit was that internal mechanism steering me from the wrongs I would have committed. In fact, I sincerely believe He kept creating escapes routes for me. All the minor accidents, near misses, gun warnings, and physical attacks I encountered were just His way of showing me that He had some greater things in store for me if I straightened up and walked within His statutes. Of course, I did not understand that at that time, but I am so thankful that He allowed me to live in order to reflect on what could have been.

As poor as we were, and as far behind and challenged as I was educationally, I am thankful God steered me toward education and not away from it. A book was as intriguing, and as valuable to me as gold and silver. An old encyclopedia was like a freshly ripened mango whose contents would be devoured in one seating. A two- or three-hundred-page book was as inviting and as entertaining as a stack of comic books.

Despite my penchant for reading, I was no nerd or book worm. I could read through twenty comic books and then go outside and throw rocks at cars. I had a devious streak in me. However, as I grew older and became more mature, I put away childish things, and focused on earning money and learning. Fortunately, that maturation guided me toward successfully reaching the ripe old age of twenty-one without an arrest, a jail sentence or worse, death. I made it there before I even realized what I had done.

Unfortunately, many young brothers in my neighborhood did not make it as they feared would be the case. My neighborhood was not unique though. Most black men growing up in poverty in urban America fear they will not make it to see age twenty-one. That's why they seem to not value other lives, or engage in activity that seriously threaten their own young lives. That's also why it is critically important for them to interact with positive black men on a very regular basis, and to avoid the situations that may contribute to a shortened lifespan. It's also important that those young brothers find as many opportunities as possible to achieve educational objectives, such as graduation from high school, workforce development programs, technical school, college, and military. I recall always telling my younger brothers how education would be the way out of the projects, and how once we earned educational accomplishments, no one could take them from us, and such education would be a ticket out of the projects and poverty.

Chapter 33

Epilogue

As an adult, things turned out okay. I graduated from college with a bachelor's degree and after completing one year of law school at FSU, I transferred to Thurgood Marshall School of Law for the final two years as planned.

During those years at Thurgood, my sister Renee died as a result of medical malpractice while she was pregnant. She was twenty-two. Four years later, my brother Tony died as a result of a gunshot to his head. He was twenty-four. A year after Tony's death, my youngest brother Travis was shot in the upper leg. Fortunately, he survived. He was twenty-four.

In the midst of all this personal tragedy, Priscilla and I had gotten married and were planning to start a family. As excited as I was about such a prospect, I feared bringing children into this world. Within a few years, however, the population boom started in the home we had purchased in the suburbs of Tallahassee.

Our first child was born in 1990 and by 1995, we had a total of four children. The stares we received whenever we went out in public were amusing. I imagined people wondering, "How could such a young mother and father have so many children?" I'm sure those thoughts as well as others, such as: "How many are his kids?" "How long will he be around?" "Is he a good father?" "Are they married?" "Is she receiving public assistance?", and so on. Whenever I saw the quizzical looks, I would give a smirk to let them know I knew what they were thinking.

Despite the lack of a strong male figure at home during my childhood, I knew what it took to be a good father, primarily, because I knew what I desired to see in a father. As such, I planned to be the best father God ever created. I planned to give my children everything I longed for but did not have. I planned to shower them with love, and to tell them every day that I loved them. I planned to encourage them, to build them up, to teach them everything about life, and most importantly teach them about Jesus Christ, and ensure they were actively involved in church and Sunday school on a very regular basis.

As a father, I developed a mindset that I would give my life for my children and at the same time, would take a life to save my children's lives. I was over-protective to a fault, especially whenever I perceived that someone perpetrated harm or even unfairness against them.

It was important to me that my children participated in as many activities as possible in order to make them as well-rounded as possible. Ballet, gymnastics, t-ball, track, soccer, basketball, football, ice hockey, cheer leading, piano, and choir were regular activities for them. We also believed it was important to get them involved in church and civic organizations, especially those organizations sponsored by my fraternity and Priscilla's sorority. I also encouraged them to compete for as many scholarship opportunities as possible, but stressed that winning was not as important as making a valiant effort.

Each of our four children went to a private Christian elementary school that Priscilla and I helped to found. The school started out in the basement of our church, and then grew to move to a much larger space. After completing elementary levels at the private school, they all went to public middle and high schools, which is where I learned to seriously sharpen my advocacy skills.

I witnessed tons of unfair treatment against my children as well as others, and spent many hours visiting schools, and on many occasions, threatening lawsuits in order to enforce their rights. At the same time, I was careful to not condone any activity of my children if I felt they did something inappropriate. I would even go as far as chastising them in front of school officials just so that the officials would clearly understand that Priscilla and I would not tolerate inappropriate or unacceptable behavior.

In one instance, the in-school behavior of one of the girls got so out of hand as far as our standards were concerned, that I decided I would quit my job and do consulting from home, so that we could take her out of the school system and home school her for her entire eighth grade year. She flourished at home while taking high-school-level courses. When she returned to school for the ninth grade, she had overachieved so greatly and had earned so many high school credits, that the school system placed her in the tenth grade as opposed to ninth. She went on to graduate with high honors, was a Presidential Scholar, went to college and graduated from a very tough business school program within four years. Had we not resorted to extreme means of taking her out of the school system and giving her individualized attention, we may have lost her to the world.

It was very clear in our household that high scholastic achievement was expected and that going to college was a no brainer. When each of the children were toddlers, we purchased pre-paid tuition plans just to ensure sufficient funds were available for each of them to attend college. We also knew we would need additional funds, and since Florida created a scholarship program from its lottery games, we knew the children had to maintain high grades in order to take advantage of those particular scholarship dollars.

I recall often telling the children that they always needed to strive to make A's because A's equaled dollars. I would give them twenty dollars for each A, and ten for each B. I gave nothing for C's because that was just a breakeven point. If they made D's or F's they would have to pay me money. I would always make it clear that although we were paying for the good grades, the big payoff would come with scholarships, and they would be reminded of that point on a regular basis.

Since I knew colleges liked students who took challenging courses, I always went over each child's schedule and encouraged them to take the more challenging courses that I knew they could handle. Sometimes, teachers or guidance counselors would not agree, but as a parent, I knew my children, and knew if they were going to be successful getting into college and taking advantage of some of the lucrative scholarship money that was available, they would need to take the more challenging courses.

Getting into rigorous courses, however, was not always easy. In one instance, one of my girls aced her English 2 Honors class in 10th grade. As far as I was concerned, the natural progression for her would have been to take an Advanced Placement English course for 11th grade. Instead, her 10th grade teacher recommended English 3 Honors. I was blown away at the recommendation that my child could not get referred to an advanced placement course, and immediately sent an email to the teacher and Assistant Principal inquiring why.

The teacher responded that my daughter was not referred because her writing skills were not great. I promptly responded that if she aced the English 2 Honors course with poor writing skills, that was a reflection of the teacher that needed to be addressed immediately. I then asked whether there were other students in the class who earned A grades but were not recommended for advanced placement. Interestingly, the teacher responded that she treated all of her students fairly and did not discriminate against any of them. I responded that I did not bring up any issue of unfairness or discrimination but thought it would be interesting if my daughter and other blacks were denied the opportunity to take the advance placement class despite mastering the honors class. The Assistant Principal promptly placed my daughter in the AP class.

In another instance, my daughter wanted to take an honors chemistry course, but was referred to a regular non-rigorous chemistry class that would not have awarded her any bonus points and no good looks from college admissions counselors. I quickly contacted the counselor, who referred me to the Assistant Principal. He advised me that due to Florida's constitutional limit of twenty-two students per classroom, he could not place my daughter in the honors class because it was full. I was very much aware of the constitutional provision, and said, "Okay, no problem, she will just take the course online through the Florida Virtual School." The Assistant Principal stated, "No, she cannot take the course through Florida Virtual School; she will have to take it here at the school." He did not know I was a lawyer, a fierce advocate for my children, especially on education–related matters, and that I knew the Florida Virtual System rules and regulations very well, because when my daughter home schooled, she took an entire year's worth of high school courses through the Florida Virtual School. I replied, "My daughter will in fact take the course through Florida Virtual School, and if the school has a problem, I suggest you contact your lawyer at the school board." After a few more exchange of pleasantries, I excused myself and advised the Assistant Principal to go ahead and drop my daughter from the regular chemistry course at school because I would register her for the Florida Virtual School course.

That same day, I registered my daughter for the honors chemistry course through Florida Virtual School. When the Assistant Principal refused to grant approval, I researched the law that indicated schools could not unreasonably withhold approval for students wishing to take classes through Florida Virtual School. I emailed it to the Principal, the Assistant Principal and the school board attorney. Approval was instantly granted for my daughter to take the course through Florida Virtual School.

I had zero advocacy or support for me when I was in school, primarily because my mother did not know how to advocate for me. She firmly believed the school officials knew best. Fortunately, I had teachers and administrators who cared for my well-being and knew that many of us poor black kids had ability and potential and would demonstrate such if given a chance. My children's situations were the exact opposite of Priscilla's and mine. Their teachers and administrators, who were almost exclusively non-black, appeared to take positions that they could not handle the rigors of a challenging academic program, or that they were not heading to college after graduation. Unfortunately, as a parent, I had to dispel those myths both inside and outside of the classroom. Priscilla and I had to maintain a constant presence at the schools, at cheerleader practices, at PTA meetings, on field trips, and during fund-raising activities, and we had to constantly challenge those who did not give our children the full benefit of the doubt, which was quite frequently. We basically had to become super-parents and outdo every other parent in fundraising and the various parent organizations, and also had to make sure our kids out-performed every other kid in every category imaginable.

A prime example of our super parent attitude was when our twin daughters did their 7th grade history projects. They had an older white social studies teacher who they did not like, and they felt she did not like them as well. Since the girls were not performing as well in the class as they should have been, I decided the history project would be the perfect time to prove to the teacher that they were two of the top students in the mostly white advanced placement class. I decided the girls would not just go to the library or the internet to read up on various civil rights matters in Birmingham, Memphis, and Little Rock. I felt we needed to go above and beyond what the other students were doing, and physically travel to those locations, visit the sites and museums, interview people, and use that information as the foundation for their reports. The lessons my girls learned from walking the halls of Little Rock's Central High School, or Birmingham's 16th Street Baptist Church, or visiting civil rights museums to see photos and videos of the angry faces of white segregationists, was more valuable than what they could have ever gotten otherwise. At least that was the argument I made to their social studies teacher before and after our trip. I needed to make sure the teacher clearly understood the girls were going well above and beyond what was necessary to complete their reports. I needed to show her that our girls could compete with the white kids. The truth of the matter is I needed to show the teacher that they had supportive parents at home who did not accept less than the absolute best. And, I needed to show my kids that they had to always be prepared to go beyond the call of duty when performing functions.

As a father, I needed to ensure that our home was a place of love, stability, safety, peacefulness, happiness, and comfort. I desperately needed to make sure my kids had what I missed out on, but so desperately craved. Family game time was important, especially family laughter where I would just act a fool and the kids would roll over with hysterical laughter. Family night out and family vacations were also regular activities for us. Whether spending Christmas in the Smokey Mountains in North Carolina, Thanksgiving at Sandestin Resort, or summer vacation in New York City, it was important that the children were exposed to as much as possible, and that we did it all together as a family.

Family worship on Sunday morning was the absolute best. There was no greater feeling for me than to rise at the sound of my 6:00 a.m. alarm on Sunday mornings, and walk through the house to get everybody up for 7:30 a.m. service, which would be followed by Sunday school. As I walked through the house, knocking on room doors saying, "Get up, rise and shine; let's go praise the Lord," I had this thing where I would talk to God, saying, "Thank you Father for selecting me to head this family. Thank you for entrusting this precious cargo to me."

After about five minutes or so, everybody would be up, and we would get dressed and get to church by 7:30 a.m. Following the morning service, we would each go to our respective Sunday school classes. Afterwards, we headed to a selected restaurant for lunch, or we would return home for my special breakfast of grits, bacon, scrambled eggs, and biscuits.

There was nothing like sitting around the breakfast table after early morning church service and laughing about what happened at church, or about the school dance the previous night, or teasing one of the kids that someone at church liked them. The fun, the laughter, and the love of family seemed so normal and so unrehearsed.

Oftentimes while we engaged in our normal family activities, my mind would drift back to those years when I was my children's age, and I would think about how I never experienced for one moment, the very moments we were experiencing at the time, and had experienced a million times before. The moment would never get lost on me that I did not have to live that sort of lifestyle as a child in order to live it with my own children. My pain had slowly turned to triumph. I started sensing a purpose in it all.

During one of those Sunday morning breakfasts, my mind drifted back to a family trip we took to Miami, when I took the family to see the big green monster, which at the time was vacant with all the windows broken and was being prepared for demolition. As I drove up to the front of the building and parked, a total silence overtook us as we all just stared at the blighted remains of a once vibrant home for hundreds of poverty-stricken black families. Finally, my oldest daughter broke the silence, and stated, "Oh my goodness, this place looks like World War II took place here!" We all got a good laugh out of that comment, but I believe for the first time in my children's lives, they got an understanding of what life was like for me when I was their age.

Later, I told Priscilla how I hoped the children gained a greater appreciation for the life we provided for them. I believe they did, but I also believe God had to show me some things in order to prepare me mentally and spiritually for what Priscilla and I needed to do to raise them such that they would not have to live that same life I lived as a youth. Were it not for those hardship experiences, I may have never learned firsthand what that type of suffering felt like. Consequently, I may not have been able to effectively witness to others in similar situations about God's grace and His mercy. So, I accept what God allowed me to go through, and quite frankly, while I did not enjoy it when I was going through it, I am happy for the experience.

It took me having to re-live my youth through this book in order for me to truly find my purpose in life. It wasn't easy; nor did I make the discovery overnight. In fact, it took a ton of prayer, reflection, and meditation. During that time, God revealed in me a greater work. I'm still not sure what that means completely, but I know it entails greater service, greater love, greater compassion, and greater humility. I will keep pressing onward toward the mark to see what's there. Through the midst of much pain, I found purpose. To God be the glory!

About The Author

Cecil Howard grew up in Miami, Florida's inner cities of Brown's Sub, Overtown and Liberty City. He discovered early in life that the key to getting out of his predicament of poverty was to get out of town and go to college.

After high school, he attended and graduated from Florda State University, where he joined Alpha Phi Alpha Fraternity, and met his future wife, Priscilla. After graduating from FSU, Cecil attended and graduated from the Thurgood Marshall School of Law at Texas Southern University.

After law school, Cecil returned to Florida and operated his own law firm focusing on civil, human and employee rights until he was recruited by a civil rights agency to lead its law department. Since then, Cecil has led several governmental and university civil rights divisions and is still actively impacting the lives of workers through his work as a diversity leader.

Cecil and Priscilla have been married over 35 years and have four adult children and two granddaughters.